OP lot 10th

North
for the
Trade

*The Life & Times
of a Berber Merchant*

North for the Trade

The Life & Times of a Berber Merchant

by John Waterbury

University of California Press, 1972

Berkeley, Los Angeles, London

UNIVERSITY OF CALIFORNIA PRESS
BERKELEY AND LOS ANGELES, CALIFORNIA

UNIVERSITY OF CALIFORNIA PRESS, LTD.
LONDON, ENGLAND

COPYRIGHT © 1972, BY
THE REGENTS OF THE UNIVERSITY OF CALIFORNIA

ISBN 0–520–02134–7
LIBRARY OF CONGRESS CATALOG CARD NUMBER: 70–174453
PRINTED IN THE UNITED STATES OF AMERICA
DESIGNED BY STEVE REOUTT

to Hadj Brahim

Contents

Preface

MUCH OF what is contained in the following pages is based on the knowledge and recollections of a single man. Like the author of these lines, I am sure that this man is fallible. Nonetheless, I have verified his reports only with regard to important events and dates in Moroccan history and major economic and social trends in Moroccan society. For more intimate or less significant facts, I have relied upon the memory of my interlocutor. Whether Hadj Brahim is in error when he claims that the French began their final assault against his homeland precisely on February 23, 1934, is less important than how he remembers it. I hope that the reader will also attune himself more to the manner in which Hadj Brahim depicts his past than to the accuracy he achieves in doing so.

Despite my efforts to simplify the text, a large number of Arabic, Berber, and French names and terms have crept in. For that reason, I have appended a list of tribe and place names and a glossary of Arabic and Berber terms. My approach to transliteration is lamentably nonsystematic although I hope that it is consistent. Expert Arabists and Berberists should have no trouble divining the roots and correct pronunciation of the transliterated words, and the nonexpert would only find tedious a proliferation of diacritical marks.

Throughout the text I have taken the precaution of fictionalizing certain personalities, including the protagonist himself, and resetting of certain events. I did this out of respect for Hadj Brahim, who sought only to help me understand the changes that he and his fellow tradesmen from the Sous have undergone. The dubious prestige of being the subject of a biography did not motivate him to cooperate with me.

The research and interviews for this study were carried out over a number of years between 1966 and 1971, usually under the umbrella of some broader research project. The Center for Near Eastern and North African Studies of the University of Michigan funded two research leaves of absence, in 1967 and again in 1970, during which the materials for this study were assembled. The Center is hereby warmly thanked for its aid and absolved of any unwanted responsibility for the views and judgments expressed in these pages. My thanks are also extended to Kenneth Brown and David Hart for their thoughtful comments and advice regarding an earlier draft of this book. Ida Altman grappled with the typing of two versions of this book; her courage and fortitude are deeply appreciated. Ellen Mandel of the University of California Press rescued the text in several instances from the impenetrable thickets into which I had driven it. I take full credit for the remaining underbrush and brambles. The map preceding the text is reproduced from International Bank for Reconstruction and Development, *The Economic Development of Morocco* (Baltimore: The Johns Hopkins Press, 1966), by permission of the publisher. The maps on page 64 are adapted from Daniel Noin, *La Population rurale du Maroc*

(Rouen: Université de Rouen, 1970), II, 191, and are reprinted by permission of the Presses Universitaires de France. Some of the photographs are used by courtesy of the Service de l'Urbanisme et de l'Habitat, Kingdom of Morocco.

Because this study focuses so closely on a single man, and, through him, on a single group, problems of placing both in the more general context of Moroccan history and society inevitably present themselves. At the outset, I shall make a brief attempt to give the reader a thumbnail sketch of Morocco.

Historically, Morocco has looked out across the Sahara to Black Africa, across the Straits of Gibraltar to Spain and southern Europe, and eastwards across Algeria to the Arab world. Her population reflects the extent to which exchanges with these areas have occurred. Before the Islamic conquests of the seventh century A.D., the inhabitants of Morocco were Berbers, an ethnic and lingual grouping whose origins are obscure and whose continuous presence in North Africa goes back to prehistoric times. This base stock has, however, been diluted by the comings and goings of many other peoples. Some have been refugees, like the Jews who trickled into Morocco following the destruction of Jerusalem in 70 A.D. More recent refugees include the many Muslims and Jews who fled southern Spain at the time of the Re-Conquest and the Inquisition. In addition, blacks from Sub-Saharan Africa, as well as ancient populations of black oasis-dwellers, have become part of the Moroccan population.

The Muslim Arab conquerors of Morocco came in small numbers but with a language and a culture that the Berbers gradually adopted. The successive dynasties of Morocco all ruled in the name of Islam. The Arab (Hillalian) invasion of the eleventh century brought a new but still limited infusion of Arab blood into Morocco. Today, the original population clearly reveals its diverse origins. There is no longer a meaningful ethnic distinction between Arabs and Berbers, although there is still an important lingual (and perhaps psychological) distinction. Berber is not a written language; Arabic is. Arabic is the language of government and intellectual life, and it is the language taught in the schools. French plays a great role in all these spheres, but it is in no way a local or indigenous language. The vast majority of the Moroccan population speaks Arabic. However, as of 1960, some 40 percent of the population still spoke Berber. To no small degree then, it appears that most of the "Arabs" of Morocco are in reality Arabic-*speakers* of Berber origins.

The Moroccan population in 1970 totaled 15,000,000. Of that population 10 percent lived in the city of Casablanca, and the cities of Rabat (the capital), Fez, and Marrakesh each had over 250,000 inhabitants. The French community of Morocco dwindled from 385,000 in 1953 to about 100,000 in 1970. In the period from 1948 to 1970 the Jewish community contracted through emigration from 255,000 to 50,000.

Morocco is a monarchy, governed by King Hassan II of the Alawite Dynasty. This dynasty has been in power since 1664, although its actual and theoretic powers were severely curtailed while the French maintained their protectorate over Morocco between 1912 and 1955. The Alawi-s trace their descent from the Prophet Mohammed. Hassan's father, Mohammed V, was exiled by the French in 1953 because he had increasingly identified himself with Moroccan nationalists seeking total independence from

France. When Mohammed V returned from exile he was venerated by the Moroccan masses as a result of his brief martyrdom. His return signaled Morocco's independence in 1956, and Mohammed V reigned from 1956 until 1961, when he suddenly died.

The Moroccan nationalists coalesced within the Istiqlal (independence) party, founded in 1944. It led the struggle for independence, a struggle that became violent after the king's exile in 1953. In the first four years of independence Mohammed V called upon many of the leaders of the Istiqlal to serve as ministers in his governments. But it soon became apparent to him that neither conservatives nor radicals within the Istiqlal shared his view that he should rule as well as reign. As a pre-emptive move, the king may have even fostered the split within the Istiqlal that gave rise to the founding of a new radical party, the National Union of Popular Forces in 1959. With the old nationalist elites fragmented, the king began to cleanse his governments of party politicians. He died before he could finish the task, but his son Hassan continued the same policies, driving the last Istiqlali ministers from the government in 1963. Heavy rioting in Casablanca in 1965 gave King Hassan the pretext to dissolve Morocco's two-year-old parliament, which he blamed for the crisis. Hassan II then ruled virtually alone for five years, until, in the summer of 1970, he ended the state of emergency that he had declared in June, 1965. A new constitution was approved by referendum, and a new unicameral parliament was elected. As laid down in the new constitution, the powers of parliament are so circumscribed as to reduce it to a docile foil for the king's policies. The recent evolution of the Moroccan polity from party-based nationalism to royal absolutism is one in which the subject of the following pages has been directly involved.

Postscript

This book was written before July 10, 1971, the date of the bloody and unsuccessful attempt undertaken by high-ranking officers of the Royal Moroccan Army to seize control of the state and eliminate many civilian associates of the King whom the officers felt were particularly sycophantic and corrupt. The coup attempt in my view was pre-emptive, led by the erstwhile bastions of military control, men who had profited greatly from an increasingly corrupt system. Those who planned the coup were executed so quickly after it failed that we will never know their exact motives. Yet it was commonly said in Morocco in the weeks following the putsch that it was obvious to the officers that graft and corruption, particularly among the civilian elite, had grown to such proportions, and was so visible to the Moroccan masses, that an explosion had become inevitable. The officers had reason to believe that young, junior officers might seek power in the name of growing popular discontent, in which case not only the King but his senior officers would be eliminated. The senior officers decided to act first. Whether they wished to overthrow the regime or bring the King to his senses cannot be known, but one can surmise that had the officers succeeded they would have undertaken a general housecleaning within the context of a rightist political outlook.

Hadj Brahim was no more than a vicarious participant in the macabre events of July 10 at King Hassan's summer palace at Skhirat. Out of that bloodbath the King emerged miraculously unscathed, but only in the physical sense. That many of the King's closest confidants could be driven to such measures, ostensibly because of civilian corruption

financed by the palace, has focussed a great deal of latent resentment among Moroccans at all social levels. The politico-
economic situation had been deteriorating for some years,
and Hadj Brahim had directly felt its repercussions in trade
at Casablanca. For those interested in what has happened at
Morocco's summit, the trademans'-eye view in Chapters III
and V may provide a helpful perspective on the impact of
elite politics beyond the confines of the capital.

Along with the rebel generals led to the stake and executed on July 13 was Commandant Manouzzi, an old com-
rade in arms of Hadj Brahim and a leader of the Moroccan
resistance prior to 1955 (see page 132). He came from a
village just down the road from Hadj Brahim's birthplace.
While Hadj Brahim has been a man of diplomacy and
politics, Manouzzi was a man of the gun. Both have been
equally faithful in their way to the cause of the Moroccan
nation. Manouzzi and his brother Said, the latter condemned
to death in September 1971 for plotting against the regime,
although unrepentant rebels, are as much sons of the Anti-
Atlas as Hadj Brahim. As declared enemies of the regime
they fought to restore in 1955, they surely represent Hadj
Brahim's alter ego, a reflection of the grocery store *jac-
querie*, one finger on the cash register and the other on the
trigger, that constituted the nervous system of the Moroccan resistance before independence.

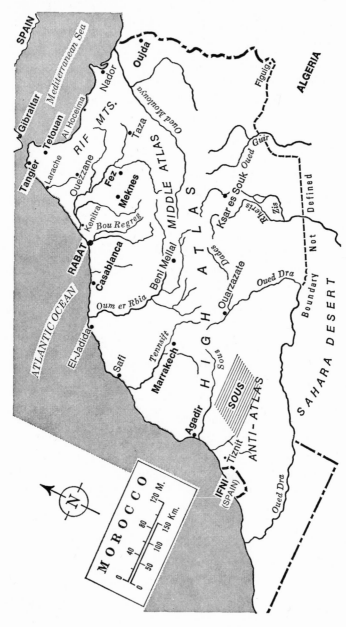

SPAIN

Gibraltar
Mediterranean Sea
Tangier
Tetouan
Al Hoceima
Nador
Larache
Ouezzane
RIF MTS.
Taza
Oujda
Oued Moulouya
Figuig
ALGERIA
Kenitra
Fez
Meknes
Bou Regreg
MIDDLE ATLAS
RABAT
Casablanca
Beni Mellal
ATLANTIC OCEAN
Oum er Rbia
El Jadida
Safi
Tensift
Marrakech
HIGH
ATLAS
Sous
SOUS
ANTI - ATLAS
Agadir
Tiznit
IFNI
(SPAIN)
Oued Dra
Ksar es Souk
Oued Guir
Rheris
Ziz
Boundary
Not
Defined
Dadès
Ouarzazate
Oued Dra
SAHARA DESERT

MOROCCO
0   40   80   120 M.
0 50 100 150 Km.

N

Redrawn from Daniel Noin, *La Population rurale marocaine* (P.U.F., Université de Rouen, 1970), 2:191.

Chapter I

------◆◆■------

Introduction

. . . if what we see is to a considerable degree a reflex of the devices we use to render it visible, how do we choose among devices?

CLIFFORD GEERTZ[1]

I DID NOT choose to write about Hadj Brahim because he is a particularly remarkable man or because his life to date has epic qualities. He *is* a remarkable man, and his life has been extremely varied and occasionally exciting. Nor did I undertake this venture because of admiration or friendship for the man. Hadj Brahim is in many ways admirable, and I genuinely like him, a feeling which he seems to reciprocate, but it would be presumptuous to claim that we are friends. To me, Hadj Brahim embodies some processes of behavior and change in Moroccan society that have held my attention over the last six or seven years, a collection of remarkable life experiences typical of what has been going on in Morocco in the twentieth century. Moreover, I suspect that the pressures to which he has been subjected, his reaction to them, and his own outlook on what he has done may be reflected in several other societies bearing roughly the same characteristics as Morocco.

In choosing my device to render Hadj Brahim and his fellows more visible, I necessarily rejected others. When I

[1] Clifford Geertz, "In Search of North Africa," *New York Review of Books*, XVI, 7 (April 22, 1971), 20.

first became intrigued by the Soussi tradesmen, I systematically accumulated a large body of socio-economic data: trade and credit statistics, proceedings of the Casablanca Chamber of Commerce, information on economic and commercial elites, all supplemented by extensive interviewing. My intention was to produce a fairly technical analysis of the Soussi trading community. But I came to the conclusion that the development of this community is too fascinating to kill off, or perhaps render invisible, through the devices commonly employed by social scientists. Moreover, I believe that there is nothing so complicated or so foreign in this group experience as to put it beyond the ken and interest of a non-specialized reader. Finally, in retrospect, I saw that I had myself learned about and developed some "feel" for the Soussi-s through the detailed recapitulation of Hadj Brahim's life. In short I decided that if this biographical device had been illuminating to me, it might well be to others. Still, that larger body of data alluded to earlier has constantly informed my treatment of Hadj Brahim's life story.[2]

In Morocco, between 1965 and 1968, I had occasion to talk with Hadj Brahim several times, and at great length, about his own career, his views on commerce and politics in Casablanca, and what the "Soussi phenomenon" means to him. He introduced me to friends and associates, escorted me about the Ammiln Valley, and took a great interest in my interest in the people from his region. On another trip to Morocco in 1970, I broached the subject of a biography with

[2] See for instance: "Les détaillants souassa à Casablanca," *Bulletin Economique et Social du Maroc*, XXXI, 114 (1969), 134–158. See also "Tribalism, Trade and Politics: The Transformation of the Swasa of Morocco," in E. Gellner and C. Micaud, *Arabs and Berbers: Ethnicity and Nation-Building in North Africa* (forthcoming, Ebenezer Baylis & Son Ltd., London, 1972).

him. His initial reaction was to shy off. "You see, Monsieur Waterbury, I am a modest man. I have done nothing unusual. My life is not very interesting. Anyhow, I don't want to attract attention to myself. . . . I don't think it would look very good." A typical Soussi, if not Moroccan, response, for too much reputation and prestige, like too much wealth, simply arouse the fear and envy of one's associates.

I reassured the Hadj that I saw him not as a unique personage but as a human being whose personal experiences might allow others to grasp more readily the impersonal trends of change in Morocco. This explanation put him at ease; he would play the role of spokesman for his tribesmates and Soussi-s in general. This, he confessed, appealed to him greatly, for he is one of those rare individuals who has thought deeply about his own life and the current of change in which he has been caught. He *analyzes* everything that goes on about him, and the idea of playing off his ideas against those of a Western "intellectual," with whom he felt at ease, attracted him.

Brahim prides himself on the breadth of his learning—which ranges from extraordinary amounts of trivia to those jarring insights that only people who have not spent twenty years in schools seem capable of producing. He knows his strengths in this respect, and quite often he would tell me, with regard to another Soussi whom I wished to see: "It's not worth it; he doesn't know how to talk." I generally checked for myself and established the accuracy of Brahim's judgment. No Soussi I have ever talked with was able to go as deeply and animatedly into a subject as Brahim. If this were not so, I probably would never have gotten myself involved in this study in the first place.

I did not have to tell him this because he knew it. "There are very few Soussi-s who know how to talk. People like to have me come to their gatherings because I know how to talk about commerce, about politics, about the world. The others aren't stupid—they could talk too, but they don't. It's the *méfiance*. Some men feel they are too important and will not deign to speak; others are too shy and don't want to make fools of themselves. But I don't have any complexes."

Hadj Brahim has a phenomenal memory for dates and figures. In this respect, I would judge that he is no more gifted than the average Soussi whose habit was, until recently, to carry all his commercial accounts in his head. When I first met him, Brahim gave me a detailed account of his career in commerce, citing exact figures and dates over a forty-year period. When I saw him again two years later, I asked him to run through the chronology again to refresh my memory. I later compared the two sets of notes and found that there was not a single discrepancy.

So it was agreed, and we met about ten times in Casablanca for two to three hours at each meeting, often terminating with a simple couscous at his apartment while he talked, listened to the news from four countries (almost a ritual with him: Spain, France, Morocco, and Algeria), and watched a Laurel and Hardy movie on television. I never met nor saw his wife, although his two young children were always present, waiting on table after their fashion, rolling on the floor in peals of laughter at the antics of Laurel and Hardy.

At the outset, I suggested that I tape our talks, but Hadj Brahim demurred: "A man's voice is his signature." Thus is lost his inimitable *sabir* French, as well as my own bastardized dialect, which he always assumed was vastly superior to his own. To the purists, I confess that I speak no *tashilhit*, the south Moroccan Berber dialect that gave rise to the name

Chleuh, the label borne by all those who speak it. Hadj Brahim, however, is perfectly fluent in French and, I would judge, perfectly at ease in it. If I lost some handle on his soul by not speaking his mother tongue, the loss is not immediately apparent to me. I would have felt surer of my grasp of his meanings had we been able to converse in *tashilhit*, but there were no feasible means available to remedy my deficiencies.

It will become evident that I have taken the liberty of trying to fit Hadj Brahim's remarks to my own interpretations of Moroccan society. This should stand as a warning to the reader, who may not share my concern with or my approach to some of the phenomena under discussion. Further, I have tried to integrate what Hadj Brahim has told me into the context of a larger body of literature and field observation dealing with his tribesmates or with groups that appear to be similar to them. This effort comes in fragments scattered throughout the book, and it is not until Chapter VII that I attempt an integrated analysis of the significance of the Soussi phenomenon in light of some recent theories of social and economic change. In short, I have not let Brahim simply speak for himself, for what is unique in his personality might obscure what is general in his experience.

The people of the Sous come in all varieties; tall or short, thin or corpulent, fair-skinned or negroid. However, there is a Soussi physical type, and Hadj Brahim represents it admirably. He is about 5'4" tall, stocky and somewhat paunchy. His salt and pepper hair is cut close to the scalp. His brown eyes dart about as he talks, and his movements, whether sitting or standing, are quick, nervous, and sometimes abrupt. He has none of the lassitude or lethargy that one associates with the bazaar merchants of Moroccan cities.

All is movement, nervous energy, quick gestures. Smiles flicker on and off his face; suddenly he lunges forward in his chair, tapping me on the knee to emphasize his remark, then catapults back in sharp, snorting laughter at the human comedy he has just described.

Brahim is fair-skinned, although I suspect that the sun would turn him quickly to a mahogany color. His face is roundish and a little jowly. Unlike many of his colleagues, he no longer wears the carefully trimmed fringe beard that seldom seems to exceed a ten-day's growth. On each of his cheeks, near the ear, are scars. These, he claims, are typical of all Swasa (pl. of Soussi). Soussi children sooner or later contract some sort of eye infection during the hot summer months (conjunctivitis?). When Hadj was young, it was believed that blood-letting reduced the infection, and the standard methods was through facial incisions.

When Hadj Brahim is in Casablanca, he invariably wears a somber business suit, a nondescript silk tie, white shirt, and a silk medallion in his lapel representing the Ordre du Trone, the Moroccan equivalent of the Légion d'Honneur. One can easily imagine him, however, in typical Soussi shop-garb: a gray or dirty-white jellaba, or baggy knee-length bloomers (*siroual*), white turban, paunch thrust forward under a grease-stained smock or work jacket, feet planted in sturdy, scruffy slippers (*babouche*). In a younger man starting off in trade, the stockiness would be absent, the smallness and quickness accentuated. Decades ago, when the Swasa first began to make an appearance in western Algeria and Paris, they were known as the "sparrows of Oran."[3]

Brahim's office is like his suit, sober and uncluttered—

[3] See Col. Justinard, "Les chleuh de la banlieue de Paris," *Revue des Etudes Islamiques*, II (1928), 478.

a steel desk, a filing cabinet, a Middle Atlas rug on the floor, two telephones, and neatly-stacked documents such as the *Official Bulletin of the Government* and monthly trade reports from the Ministry of Commerce. There is not a hint of his past. From this office, he directs the Moroccan Union of Wholesalers of Food Products, which, despite its ecumenical title, groups, for the most part, Soussi tea and sugar wholesalers. His business, to which he devotes only part of his time nowadays, is one among several wholesale depots on the Route de Strasbourg. Like the rest, it is stacked high with tins of cooking oil, crates of tea, and sacks of sugar cones.

His apartment is also notable for the lack of clues it gives one to his origins. It is not far from his office, just a few steps away from the Route de Strasbourg. The first time I visited the merchant there was shortly after he had moved in. Before letting us in, Hadj Brahim banged on the door, then opened it and shouted down the corridor in *tashilhit* what was clearly a warning to the womenfolk to keep out of sight. Then he took me to the bathroom, a large pink-tiled affair, which he showed me with considerable pride. At the end of the corridor was a large living room where the Hadj apparently slept, although there were also a couple of bedrooms. On the floor of the livingroom was what amounted to wall-to-wall carpeting, one half of which was blue and the other green, separated by a red band. Low couches with mattresses, that one finds in almost all Moroccan homes, ran along two walls, covered with a peach-colored brocade. Some inlaid tea-tables were scattered about, as were a couple of formica-topped tables. On top of one was a stack of hand towels used to dry off one's hands after washing them both before and after eating, and on another was placed a tea set. Two chairs and a couch, covered in black and red artificial

leather, confronted an enormous television set that com-
pleted the ensemble. Hadj Brahim's mock ferocious commands to his children in *tashilhit* and the appearance of
argan oil on the table where we ate the couscous were the
only reminders that I was with a man from the Anti-Atlas
mountains.

It may well be Hadj Brahim's chameleon-like ability to
take on the mental and physical color of his surroundings
without rejecting his own core identity that has intrigued
me. He is at once a humble mountain man and world travel-
er; a city merchant and a simple tribesman; a pious, sometimes simplistic Muslim, and a canny politician at home in
the politics of a new nation. Like any Moroccan his age,
Brahim has had a broad range of experience in his lifetime.
The two major protagonists of Morocco's traditional system
—the sultanate and the tribe—have been restructured or dissolved by colonial administration and economic integration;
Hadj Brahim has participated in the last gasps of tribal dis-
sidence and the birth of modern political movements in
Morocco. His mind has made and stored a running commentary on the changes arising from the colonial impact.
He, like many of his countrymen, is the "transitional man"
about whom so much is written and so little understood.

Whether anyone can agree on the relative importance,
strength, and function of groups in Morocco, an analysis of
Moroccan society inevitably grapples with the problem of
understanding individual behavior in terms of group affili-
ation. This is hardly surprising, and the reader will probably
realize that I am concerned with tribes, families, religious
sects and orders, guilds, and regional or ethnic groupings—
in sum, the full panoply of ascriptive categories to which
we habitually resort in looking at "developing societies."

There are political parties, unions, and interest groups too—bodies defined by function rather than blood, race, or religious belief—although the practical distinction is at times difficult to make. There may also be today a strong trend toward atomization, toward the breakdown of traditional group frameworks, the development of nuclear family units, and the freeing of the individual from group restraints—or is the individual simply set adrift?

The latter process nothwithstanding, up to the present time Moroccans have organized their social, political, and economic activities in terms of adherence to some sort of group. These groups, and the way people relate to them, have undergone substantial change in this century. It is precisely in this respect that the recent history of the tribes of the Anti-Atlas mountains—the people known as the Soussi-s—became for me such an attractive subject for study. Individual Soussi-s have been born into a tribal society that fits most of our notions of "traditionalism." Their way of life was deeply shaken only in the past few decades, and this at the hands of the French, who did not come to Morocco in force until 1912, and did not conquer all of the Sous region until 1934. Living Swasa have experienced the loss of local autonomy built around the tribes, as the French gradually extended their central administrative system to cover the entire territory in the name of the French protectorate. During this time, many Swasa emigrated from the region, seeking their fortune elsewhere as miners, as workers in French munitions factories in the First World War, and as retailers in the northern cities of Morocco. This trend had started a generation before the coming of the French, but it was only after the First World War that the Swasa found themselves sucked into the nascent national market economy that grew with the French presence. Finally, these same Soussi-s lived on into the era of national independence after 1955, rising to new heights in the commercial networks of Moroccan cities.

Through all this, the Swasa operated in the group context. What that context means to them and how it has changed are illustrated by the life and views of Hadj Brahim and of some of his fellow Soussi-s. Some phenomena that I wish to explore are: the ambivalence that permeates individual and group ties in Moroccan society; the concomitant balance between intense, introverted rivalries and the pressures to maintain group solidarity; the nature of group identity and how those inside view those outside; how individuals and groups have adapted to the political and economic pressures of contemporary Morocco; and, finally, how we may relate the experience of the Swasa to entrepreneurship, economic development and social change.

Someone like myself, who has been immersed in the increasingly technical, jargonized language of the social sciences, may find it difficult to write simply and clearly about what appear to be, and are, hideously complex situations. At the same time that I attempt to honor the canons of simple, expository prose, I feel obligated to make a scholarly contribution, to refer to, and take up disciplinary issues that may interest only the specialist. How my reading of Moroccan behavior relates to Festinger's theory of cognitive dissonance, or Coser's on the functions of conflict, may have meaning only for a small audience. So too, but for a different audience, Brahim's analysis of the tribal confederations of Tahuggwa and Tagazzoult, much beloved of the late French ethnographer, Robert Montagne. Such remarks are intended for the social scientist and the Moroccanist; they need not retain the attention of the reader who is neither. On the other hand, the very notion of using one man to illustrate facets of social change may appear to the social scientist to lead, fatally, to superficiality and distortion. In all likelihood, I will irritate the non-specialist and specialist alike. I offer my apologies to both.

Of course there is Brahim himself, a man well worth our attention whether or not his experiences are representative of those of his countrymen. I am convinced, nonetheless, that, although he may be more articulate than many of his fellows, his personal views on human conduct and on his place in the divine order of things are not atypical. I intend to explore Hadj Brahim's approach to entrepreneurship, his "ethic" in the Weberian sense of the word, and his motivation in David McClelland's scheme of things. At times, as we shall see, Brahim's remarks place him squarely in the tradition of the Protestant ethic, or, in more clinical terms, he professes many of the values of the high n-achiever. At other moments, he is the archetype Muslim fatalist, yielding to a destiny that God alone shapes.

It is difficult to pigeonhole Brahim, or anyone like him. As soon as we seem to have a hold on his motivations, on what makes him tick, he develops another line of thought in *seeming* contradiction; the confusion is in our minds—or in my mind—not in his. This is but another aspect of the ambivalence that runs through human behavior in Morocco, and it is an ambivalence recognized by Moroccans themselves. It is reflected in their constant awareness of the *provisionality* of everything; the fragility of wealth, of friendship, of love, of hate, of peace, war, the regime, and of life itself. All is provisional and fragile save Islam, which describes and analyzes the ambivalence of man's relations with other men, but provides him with the faith, and in Brahim's case, the serenity, that enable him to cope with his fate here on earth.

Chapter II

The Valley

In a photograph taken from an American space capsule, the Anti-Atlas Mountains of southwestern Morocco look as desolate as the surface of the moon.[1] Yet when one visits these mountains, which rise in places to eight or nine thousand feet, the impression is different. The upper slopes are undeniably barren, eroded, and dessicated, but one constantly comes across small valleys and pockets of verdure, groves of almond and olive trees, miniscule fields of barley, or scattered *argan* trees shading green patches of meadow grass. In February and March, when the almond trees are in blossom and the water courses winding down the sides of the mountains are full from the winter rains, the high valleys of the Anti-Atlas are extraordinarily beautiful and seemingly prosperous. Nonetheless, it is the photo from space that tells the truth.

The entire region suffers from lack of rain; seldom do more than twelve to sixteen inches a year fall, the minimum for any kind of agriculture. The sedentary tribal populations that have lived continuously in the area for at least three centuries have gradually reduced the meager resources even further through overgrazing of the natural ground cover, hacking down the *argans* for wood, depleting the soil, and

[1] See the *National Geographic*, XXX, 4 (November, 1966), 656–657.

watching a good deal of it wash or blow away. It is, however, an agricultural area, fairly densely inhabited, with an average of forty people per square kilometer.

The inhabitants have never been able to depend entirely upon local resources for their survival. For as long as anyone can remember or as far back as records date, the people of the Sous have tapped resources outside their area, such as the trans-Saharan trade which was channeled from black Africa through the Bani oases to the south of the mountains, or along the Atlantic coast, the Tazeroualt, and in more recent times through the cities of Agadir, Taroudant, and Mogador. During periods of famine or prolonged drought, entire populations might abandon their fields and temporarily swarm north to the Atlantic coastal plains, where chances for survival seemed better. In the last century or so individual males have pushed off to the north, leaving their families behind. Some earned their way as *tulba*, the men of religion and a modest level of learning who would teach the Koran to the children of northern villages. When the French developed western Algeria, some Soussi-s went there to work in the mines. Others broke into petty trade in the great traditional cities of the north—at Fez, Salé, and Marrakech.

Population growth and the arrival of the French in this century accelerated the process, as did the famine years of 1879 to 1885, 1926, 1936, and 1945.[2] In this century the inhabitants of the Anti-Atlas developed the characteristics of other sedentary populations noted for their commercial prowess or capacity for hard manual labor throughout the

[2] Some estimates indicate that half the population may have died from famine between 1879 and 1885. There was a virtual exodus of the survivors toward the north. See J.-L. Miège, *Le Maroc et l'Europe* (Paris, 1962), III, 443.

Middle East: the Riffis, the Mzabis, and Kabyles of Algeria, the Djerbans of Tunisia, the Lebanese, the Hadramawtis, and others. In schematic form, over a half-century temporary male migration out of the Anti-Atlas became the norm. This migration initially filled the gap in a deficient agricultural system. By the Second World War the resources earned by the migrants were easily as important as those produced in the home valleys, and in the ten years following the war commerce or labor in the north became the dominant activity of virtually all able-bodied males. Agriculture took a position of decidedly secondary importance. The prosperity that one finds today in several areas of the Anti-Atlas was imported.

Agricultural conditions in Morocco still affect inhabitants of the area, but now there is an intervening step. In Morocco 70 percent of the population depends on agriculture for a livelihood, and when crops are bad the whole economic system suffers. The thousands of petty tradesmen who have gone north are faced with customers who want to buy and postpone payment. The home valleys immediately feel the loss of income in a bad agricultural year, even though migration has freed the mountain populations from the direct impact of *local* agricultural conditions.

Hadj Brahim is from the Anti-Atlas mountains and is, among other things, a wholesaler in Casablanca. He and thousands of others like him in Morocco's cities are called Soussi-s or Chleuhs or both. In fact, Hadj Brahim was for years known as Brahim as-Soussi and this was the name he had printed on his first business cards. The people from this region are called Soussi-s because they live in vague proximity of the Wad Sous, a river which divides the Anti-Atlas from the High Atlas and flows into the sea just south of Agadir. Few of the Soussi-s one encounters in the north live in the river valley, but rather in the mountains lying to the south.

They are also called Chleuh because the Berber dialect they speak is known as *shilha* or *tashilhit*. However, this dialect is not restricted to the Anti-Atlas and is spoken in much of the High Atlas also. But when Moroccans talk about Soussi-s, they generally mean people from a much more restricted population. The thousands of petty tradesmen that have infiltrated the northern cities have been spewed forth by five or six tribes installed on the slopes of a massive and beautiful mountain, the Jebel Lkist. For the record, the tribes in question are the Ammiln, the Ida ou Gnidif, the Ait Baha, the Ait Mzal, the Ida ou Ktir, and the Ait Souab. There are others, but none of them was ever so totally absorbed by petty trade in the north as those just mentioned. Within this small cluster of tribes, representing perhaps 70,000 people, one stands out above all others for their skill, success, and commitment to trade. That tribe is the Ammiln.

Hadj Brahim was born into the Ammiln in 1914, two years after the establishment of the French protectorate in Morocco, but twenty years before the French conquered his valley. His birthplace, Iskouzrou (the top of the rock) is really an agglomeration of three villages (*muda'*). The people known as the Ammiln (14,500 souls in 1960[3]) live in a

[3] Population estimates from 1936 and more reliable census figures from 1960 would indicate that while the birth rate in the Sous may be the same as for the rest of Morocco (i.e., ca. 3.3 per cent per annum) there has been little population growth in the region, presumably because so many Swasa are resident in the north. Thus the population of the Ammiln was estimated at 14,415 in 1936 and 14,547 in 1960. The total population of the core tribes appears to have increased from 54,000 to 67,000 over the twenty-four year period. The most thorough study of the population of the area over time is to be found in Daniel Noin, *La Population rurale du Maroc*, 2 vols. (Rouen: PUF, 1970). In 1965 he estimated the density in the

valley of the same name that stretches along the southern slopes of the Jebel Lkist. The Ammiln are not a tribe in the sense that all people in the valley claim descent, fictive or otherwise, from common ancestors. They are a cluster of seven tribes, each founded on blood descent, but whose members accept and even employ a geographic designation to define themselves vis à vis outsiders. Thus, whenever I refer to "tribe" in the following lines, I have in mind one of the seven groups that constitute the Ammiln, but not the Ammiln in the aggregate. Brahim was born into the tribe known as the Afelli-wasif, "the people who live upstream." As one might guess there is another tribe known as "the people who live downstream" (Agounsi-wasif). It is only at a lower level of tribal organization that one encounters genea-logically-defined units, the *afus* (pl. *ifassen*) or "hands," whose members claim descent from a common ancestor. The *afus* is a clan.

The Ammiln valley is elongated, as is the mountain it-self. The Lkist looms eight thousand feet in barren splendor, dominating the entire valley strung out at its feet. Like the Grand Canyon, the Lkist has a life of its own, going through, from dawn to dusk, an arresting series of improvisations on its basic ochre hue.

The valley itself is not very broad, hardly more than a few miles, and is about eleven miles long. It slopes gently from north to south. A string of villages runs along the northern edge of the valley, where the rocky slopes of the Lkist meet the first cultivated fields and groves of trees. A second string of villages runs along the southern reaches of

---

Ammiln valley to be 120 (!) per km² as compared to the regional average of 40 (I, 173). He also argues that population density in the Anti-Atlas may have been the same or even higher in the sixteenth century than it is today (p. 175).

the valley. Iskouzrou is in the upper chain. Between the two chains is fairly open ground, broken up by clumps of argan trees and date palms and used for raising barley and for pasturage for animals (almost exclusively goats). Now that agriculture is of less than vital concern to the Ammiln, the houses of the tradesmen are gradually moving out into the fields. The villages are situated along the water courses, wadis, and around springs that originate on the Jebel Lkist. Along the streams elaborate terracing has created miniscule, irrigated fields and dense groves of almond and olive trees.

The regulation of water distribution was a major aspect of tribal life and introduced a certain ambivalence into the very notion of belonging to a tribe. For the tribe was above all an instrument to defend the resources of its members, and as long as its members identified strongly with it, their defense was fairly sure. But if geography forced them to share their resources with other tribes, tribes with whom they might occasionally have to fight over questions of women for instance, then the whole problem of enmity had to be treated with great circumspection. The people who lived downstream could not afford to be too chauvinistic vis à vis the people who lived upstream lest they lose their water. The people upstream could not afford to be cavalier with the water at which they had first crack lest they be denied access to the fields in the lower valley. What tribal identity put asunder, resource sharing drew together. In a general way, we will find this theme repeated constantly in the life of Hadj Brahim and his associates, be it in the valley or in the commercial arena of Casablanca.

The major administrative center of the Ammiln is in the small town of Tafrawt, which does not lie in the valley itself but slightly to the south, on a rocky plateau that forms the southern wall of the valley. It is the site of an important

Wednesday market, held there since long before the French arrived in the area. The other major market is on Sundays at the village of Tahala, some eight miles to the south, and the center of one of the tribes of the Ammiln. It was, until recently, the home of one of the several Jewish communities scattered through these mountains, some of whose members claim descent from refugees of the destruction of Jerusalem in 70 A.D. The two hundred or so Jews of Tahala left the village and Morocco in the years after 1956, apparently to emigrate to Israel.

The villages on the plateau or shelf of Tafrawt are dense clusters of houses on the curious, smooth, pink granite rock formations that have long attracted tourists to the region. Although these rock formations are not as common in the valley itself, the basic contours of the villages are everywhere alike. They are built along the steep rock slopes of the mountain where agriculture is difficult. To conserve space the houses are packed in wall-to-wall, or roof to wall as they climb the hill. Despite the proximity of these houses, great care is taken to construct them in such a manner that one household cannot spy upon the activities of any of the others —above all, so that the activities of the women cannot be observed by males in another house. In recent years, now that successful merchants have begun to build individual houses apart from the old village clusters, it has often required long periods of negotiation—in one instance seven years—for the would-be builders to overcome the villagers' suspicions that the new house was really designed to give its occupants a better vantage point to violate the privacy of the others. This obsessive concern with the privacy of one's womenfolk contrasts with the lack of concern implied in the claim that it is unusual for anyone to lock the door of his house.

The houses themselves are solidly constructed in stone and mortar, frequently covered with an ochre plaster. Most often they have three stories, the first floor being used for the animals, grain storage, milling, and cooking, and the upper two stories for living and eating quarters. Windows in the outer walls are narrow slits, used for observation and, during a feud, for shooting, rather than for light and air, which are supplied by an interior well from roof to ground floor. On the outside, an ornamental door frame, unique to this region, spreads its black and white design far up the wall over the wooden entrance door.[4] Today, increasingly, the houses are concrete with large exterior windows. The utility lines disappearing into their walls indicate to outsiders that their owners have "made it."

Iskouzrou has yet to be invaded by this new architecture. It is one of the oldest village agglomerations in the valley, according to Brahim, although he at once points out that its inhabitants, like virtually all Swasa, came from the fabled oasis town of Tamdoult. They fled Tamdoult, which lay at the edge of the Sahara Desert (near present-day Akka), after an earthquake destroyed it.

Tamdoult was near a rich silver mine which made the town's fortune in the flourishing trans-Saharan trade of the medieval period. Its destruction occurred in the sixteenth century. Whether caused by earthquake, as the Hadj would have it, or at the instigation of the leader of a powerful tribe, the Mejjat, is less important than the widely held Swasa belief that God wished to punish its inhabitants for their hard-heartedness. Some French scholars suggest that the

[4] See André Adam, "La maison et le village dans quelques tribus de l'Anti-Atlas," *Hespéris*, XXXVII (1950), 289–362. 3rd ed., 4th trim.

destruction of Tamdoult triggered a movement of the oasis populations toward the Anti-Atlas mountains to the north. As the newcomers moved into the mountains, they encountered populations that were none too eager to absorb them. Two large "confederations" of the indigenous and the invading populations emerged from this, or so the theory goes, known as Tahuggwa and Tagazzoult.[5] They were, according to Robert Montagne, supratribal alliances (Arabic *leff*; Berber *amqun*) through which a tribe in one alliance could mobilize support for warfare against a tribe in the other alliance. Another indication of the ambivalence inherent in group relations in the Sous—and a fact that Montagne apparently overlooked—is that these alliances cut *across* tribes, with clans within the same tribe joining different alliances. This was the case with the Ammiln. The extent to which the alliances ever functioned is difficult to ascertain, and they are a distant and fading memory for most Swasa today.

Hadj Brahim, who is fairly strong on the history of his area, is convinced that Tahuggwa and Tagazzoult, whatever their origins, were simply devices by which the old Moroccan sultanate, far away to the north beyond the High Atlas Mountains, would try to control the Sous. It was the old tactic of divide and rule; the tribes of Tagazzoult were suitably rewarded by the Sultan for submission to the Sultan's government (the *makhzen*), and those of Tahuggwa fought for local independence. Hadj Brahim pointed out that all these machinations were particularly virulent in the nineteenth century, and summed up that it was no wonder

[5] On Tamdoult, see Col. Justinard, *Notes sur l'histoire du Sous au XVIe siècle*, Archives Marocaines, Paris, XXIX (1933), 79–82; and Vincent Monteil, "Choses et gens du Bani," *Hespéris*, XXXIII (1946), 398, 3rd–4th trim. The theory of the two great Anti-Atlas confederations is developed in Robert Montagne, *Les Berbères et le Makhzen dans le Sud du Maroc* (Paris, 1930).

that the French were so fascinated by the alliances, for they hoped to divide and rule the Sous like the Sultans before them.[6]

The standard explanation that one hears in the Sous of the origins of Tahuggwa and Taggazoult is indicative of the introverted nature of their conflicts. One of Hadj Brahim's friends, the major wholesaler of Tafrawt, once told me that one could be sure of at least one thing: that behind every conflict there is a woman, and that the two tribal confederations are no exception. The Hadj himself offers the following: two wives were married to the same husband, and the sons of each founded lineages that divided the Sous. Indeed, in the recent history of the area, rivalries between brothers and half-brothers are a frequent theme of which Tahuggwa and Tagazzoult may offer the archetype. Beyond this, the valley was periodically, perhaps constantly, feud-ridden.

"Before 1934 we had liberty in anarchy in the Sous. There was not much security. The feud was particularly rampant in the years just before the coming of the French. I remember that when I was a young man the first profits I earned in trade at Tangier went into the purchase of a rifle. Of course I wanted the rifle to fight the French. But you know lots of young men were doing the same thing, and you have to test your rifle before using it in earnest. So there was a lot of shooting in the valley."

The feud was the product of the inner tensions of the sedentary society of the Sous, tensions aggravated, if not caused, by the pressure of the population upon its own narrow resource base. The resources of families, villages and tribes were and are transferred through the male line. Wom-

[6] In the past the tribes of the Ammiln were distributed as follows. Tagazzoult: Ait Smayoun, Afelli-wasif and half of Amanouz. Tahuggwa: Tahala, Tafrawt, Agounsi-wasif, and half of Amanouz.

en represent the weak link in the chain in that through them outsiders—intruders—can gain access to those resources through marriage and inheritance. The conduct of women is subject to constant surveillance, a matter of obsessive concern, in direct relation to the feeling of vulnerability they introduce among the males of the lineage (the agnates). Behind every feud, then, there is a woman; but women are an excuse more than a cause. Moreover in any given instance of feud the outsider can perhaps discern no specific causes other than the fears and anxieties of the participants themselves.

The feud was endemic although not very costly in lives. André Adam, who lived at Tafrawt during the Second World War, recalls discovering that his gardener had once been a renowned hired assassin, somebody's paid gun in the feuds of the first decades of this century. Adam then recounts the story of a feud in which one faction dug tunnels under the house of their rivals, packed in some charges of gun powder, and set them off on the wedding day of a rival tribesman.[7] I mentioned Adam's account to Hadj Brahim to have his reaction. One of his quick smiles flickered across his face. "Of course! You know, that assassin, he came from our *muda'*, Iskouzrou. And the marriage, that too took place in our village.

"It is a long and complicated story, but as you know, Iskouzrou was really three villages joined together. There was Assis, in which I lived, Tazoult, and Iskel. Each of these villages is divided into hands, *ifassen*, such as my own, the Ait Hsain. At some point all of Iskouzrou became divided between two leagues of *ifassen*. One league was called Ait Bilq, and my *afus*, the Ait Hsain, were part of it. The other league was called Ait Talib. So not only was Iskouzrou di-

[7] Adam, *Hespéris.*

vided into three villages but into two factions as well [see Figure 1]. At one point the two factions had separate cemeteries and mosques.

"In any case things were very bad between Ait Talib and Ait Bilq before the French came. No one knows when the feud first broke out, but it can't be too old. I've been told that some time ago there was a man who had six brothers, and he disputed with them. Then he went off to al-Jadida for the trade. Instead of leaving his brothers to keep an eye on his wife, he delegated this task to some 'strangers' [people outside his *afus*]. That was very insulting to the brothers, who were furious. The man's wife had a child,

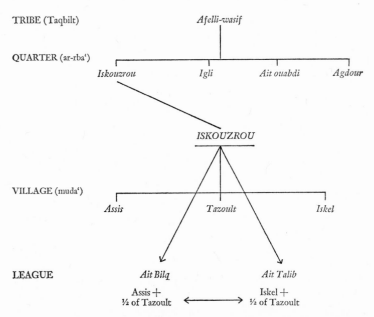

Tribal Levels among the Ammiln

NOTE: David Montgomery Hart, who also talked with Hadj Brahim at length, kindly communicated his diagram of village alignments which correspond to that above. Letters of 11/12/68 and 31/12/68.

and on the name-day[8] she invited her husband's brothers to come to the celebration. They refused, and that was even more insulting. The husband had to defend his honor. The feud broke out among the brothers and divided the entire village. There were many incidents that followed over the years, including the one when the marriage reception was sabotaged. From time to time there would be a truce when the *shurfa* [men claiming descent from the Prophet Muhammad] came to negotiate peace in the name of Islam—for a fee, of course."

Hadj Brahim went on to speak in general about the feud. "If there was a murder and the killer was known, he had to go into exile. The tribe would decree him an exile. This meant that the family of the murdered man could not take vengeance on the members of the killer's family. Five members of the victim's family would be declared in writing as the official avengers, and they could track down the assassin and kill him. If that happened, they would not be exiled from the tribe themselves. If the original killing was involuntary, the killer could pay blood money [*diya*] to the victim's family. Sometimes, even if the killing was voluntary, the tribe could pardon the assassin.

"Of course there were killings where the assassin was not known. I remember hearing a story about such a murder. The son of the dead man went to the mosque and fired two shots to signal a meeting of the *ifassen*. When they were all assembled, the son came before them and announced his father's murder. He thanked the men for coming but added that they could all go home for he had just seen the killer among them. At this point the killer, thinking that he had been identified, jumped up and tried to run away.

[8] Muslim children receive their name on the seventh day after birth.

"Often there were not enough tricks to unmask the killer. People would accuse one another of the crime, and a man's blood relatives would have to swear to his innocence. This would happen for any crime that went unexplained. Sometimes five members of his *afus* would swear for him, at others twelve, and at others twenty-five. For murder the man accused needed fifty members of his *afus* to support him. Only the men of his *afus* would do this. Generally the swearing [*thagalit*] took place at the tomb of a saint [a *sidi* or what the French call a *marabout*] with a *fqih* [a man sufficiently learned in Islam to teach] presiding and holding the Koran."

Conflict in the Sous could occur at just about any level of social organization. No unit could be characterized as cohesive. In fact, each unit—the family, the *afus*, the village, the tribe, and non-blood alliances—served not to prevent conflict but to cope with it when it broke out. No group provided that security which would enable a man to say "here, I need fear nothing," and consequently no group could evoke the total commitment of its members. In other words, the Soussi could see his universe as peopled by potential allies and potential enemies, the same people playing either role according to the situation at hand. There was nothing immutable about friendships and enmities, for they were situational phenomena, and a change in the contours of any given conflict could bring about a dramatic reversal of roles. A man might try to kill one of his own agnates in a village feud, and then find himself obliged to call on his would-be victim to swear to his innocence when accused of a crime in another village or *afus*.[9]

[9] I have tried to analyze this problem of "dissonance" in relation to other aspects of Moroccan behavior. See my *The Commander of the Faithful—the Moroccan Political Elite*. (New York:

The unit best equipped to deal with tension and con-flicts was the *afus* or "hand." The *afus* might have as many as fifty families in it. A family is known as a "hearth" (*takat*, pl. *kanoun*), and no levels of organization (such as the *ighs* or fingers in other Berber tribes) intervene between the fam-ily and the *afus*. There might be several *afus* in a village—at Iskouzrou there were thirteen. Each *afus*, or perhaps the village itself, would have a leader, generally chosen for life (the *anfugour*; pl. *infugourn*). "He was generally an aged man so that serving for life was perhaps only a matter of a few years. But we have great respect for the wisdom of the elderly. What the *anfugour* did was to act as an arbiter in disputes within the *afus* and also to levy fines [*tafgurt*]. For instance, if someone let his goats wander into another man's fields, or if there was a theft or problems over water, the *anfugour* would handle them.

"For the tribe, there was the leader known as *anflous* [pl. *inflassen*], who did just about the same thing. The tribe was usually divided into quarters [*l'rba*] and each quarter would have an *anflous* [also see Figure 1]. Each tribe had its code [*luh*: literally a piece of wood] which set down all the fines for misdemeanors and the regulations for the local mar-ket. The *anflous*, advised by the men of the tribe, would see to it that the *luh* was applied. Only married men who had founded a hearth could participate in these councils. Every-thing had a price, even insults. If a man was wounded, his wound would be measured by the fingers of an average-sized man, and the *luh* would say how much each finger was worth according to the nature of the wound. The *ifassen* still exist

Columbia University Press, 1970), and Waterbury and Vinogradov, "Situations of Contested Legitimacy; Morocco—An Alternative Framework," in *Comparative Studies in Society and History*, XIII, 1 (January, 1971).

today and so do the *inflassen*, although not officially of course. They still look after the upkeep of the mosque and the feeding and upkeep of the *tulba* [religious instructors]. The government has appointed its own local men, the *shaykh-s* and the *muqaddim-s*. But no one wants that job; they're no better than letter carriers [*rqass*]

"Before the French came we fought all the time, but we had two rules that no one ever violated. We would never tolerate any prostitution among our women, and no matter what we did to ourselves, we would never harm a hair on the head of a Jew. The French brought in some prostitution to Tafrawt from outside, but there was little we could do about that. Even today, none of our women would ever go to market. The only women that are permitted to do so are widows. And even then the most respectful of them would wait a few kilometers outside the market until an elderly man whom they knew would come by on his donkey. They would ask him to buy for them what they needed, and then they would wait all day until he came back from the market with their purchases."

The Soussi-s are well-known for their puritanical attitude toward their women, although an incident that I will relate further on suggests that there are many nuances to this image. It is curious in the Ammiln valley to see that women are allowed to work the fields—a necessity, given that their men are in the north—but they do so veiled, one corner of the long black shawl they wear pulled entirely across their face. A sidewise glance at a stranger passing by is occasion for a good deal of verbal abuse on the part of the young boys or old men who have been left behind to look after them. All this, Brahim laments with his customary resignation, is changing rapidly.

Some mention has already been made of the fact that

there were ancient Jewish settlements in the Anti-Atlas Mountains.[10] They were active in several walks of life. They made practically all the silver and gold jewelry for which the area is noted. Some communities in the Bani oases at the northern edge of the Sahara, and in the Tazeroualt region, once the center of a flourishing kingdom, were active in trans-Saharan trade. Others worked with Jewish merchants at Mogador (now Essaouira) on the Atlantic coast, which exported products of the Sous to Europe. Jews, scattered through the mountains, would help buy up the annual almond harvest and deliver it to Mogador for export. Finally there were the more humble professions that involved repairing various instruments used by the Soussi-s in local agriculture. The Jews, according to Islam, are a protected people (dhimmi, as are the Christians). They could bear no arms and thus, in a very practical sense, needed to have a Muslim "protector" who would answer, with arms if necessary, for their safety.

Hadj Brahim is convinced of the good treatment of the Jews that lived among the Ammiln, above all at Tahala.[11] "We never touched the Jews; in all our fighting they were always protected. They lived much better than us. They ate wheat when we ate barley; they ate eggs when all we had was goat's milk. I don't know why they all left. But probably it's because every Jew thinks he will go straight

[10] See Pierre Flamand, Les communautés israélites du Sud-Marocain (Casablanca, n.d.; 1951?).

[11] The mellah at Tahala may have been established about 1550. There may have been other such mellah-s in the area as well. One such mellah, Tatelt, in the tribe of the Ida ou Milk in the Ammiln Valley itself, was apparently razed and its inhabitants dispersed in 1840. See Jean Chaumeil, "Le mellah de Tahala au pays des Ammeln," Hespéris, XL (1953), 227–240.

to paradise if he dies in Jerusalem." There are no more Jews today at Tahala. All left following the end of the French protectorate in 1956. Now their houses are inhabited by blacks from the southern oases.

"There have been people coming up here from the oases—from the Bani—as long as anyone can remember. They come during hard times in large numbers, but there has always been a trickle. We use them to build houses and to work our fields. Even though they are black, they are Chleuh just like us. We are all the same. Before, they had the status of slaves. But we always treated them very well and they continued to come. We liberated them as prescribed by the Koran, and there are now whole communities of them who live just like us."

One of Hadj Brahim's contemporaries had a somewhat different view. I was standing with this man on the main square at Tafrawt. A couple of blacks were lethargically filling in a hole in the road. My companion, as if provided with a script straight from Biloxi, complained, "Look at them! They're so lazy, it'll take them all day to fill in that hole. And besides they smell. Every year there are more and more of them. That's all you see in the markets now. I don't know what this place is coming to!"

The Swasa, although not always practicing their religion to the letter, pride themselves on their piety and devotion to Islam. Long before the area became known for its retailers, it had a reputation for exporting teachers of religion: *tulba* (sing. *talib*). The men of religion have always been a force that linked the Sous to the Sultanate to the north and, in a far broader sense, to the Islamic community as a whole. They represent a universalist element that complements the particularism and isolation of the region. Through their knowledge of Arabic, and hence the Koran, they maintained that fascination for the written text and the legal deed characteristic of the Chleuh.[12] Brahim marveled at the zeal of the Ammiln *tulba*, who at one point wanted to change all the place names of the valley from Berber to Arabic. "Can you imagine that when they drew up legal deeds, they always wrote "qimma as-sakhra" (top of the rock) rather than Iskouzrou!"

"We never produced as many tulba as some of the other tribes, but every village had its mosque [*timzgida*] and its Koran school for the children. The *tulba* in the village are responsible for the education of the children in Koran, for leading the prayers at the mosque, and for drawing up and notarizing acts. At the next level, practically every tribe had its own religious school [*madersa*]. There are five in all in the Ammiln.[13] The boy who had learned the Koran by heart might go on to the *madersa* to study the Arabic language: grammar, composition, and syntax. Then he would study Islamic law [*shari'a*], personal status, and *hadith*. It was a very difficult life for the *tulba*. They lived in tiny cubicles at the *madersa* and they didn't have much to eat. They were paid out of the tithe ['*ashur*] that was collected each year on agricultural produce, and if there was a drought they practically starved. It is still very difficult for them. Even a shepherd lives better than a *talib*. At the *madersa* of the Afelli-wasif there are only nineteen *tulba* now."

[12] See for instance Jacques Berque, *Structures sociales du Haut-Atlas* (Paris: PUF, 1955), pp. 335–336.

[13] Today there is a public primary school at Tafrawt. But to go any higher, pupils must go to the secondary school at Tiznit. My impression is that the children who are being educated go to schools in the cities of the north rather than in the mountains.

When the *talib* has written the chosen verses on the wooden writing board, he gives it back to the pupil and teaches him how to read it before moving on to the next pupil. The pupil begins to pronounce it aloud, chanting, and rocking back and forth.

The *talib* sets all his pupils in motion in this manner, one after the other, then, with his long switch, now standing in their midst, now listening and trying to pick up an error of pronunciation of a single pupil among all the others, or again sitting next to one who is reciting poorly and repeating the verse with him without losing track of the others, he succeeds in orchestrating an interminable psalmodie that would seem an atrocious cacaphony to the uninitiated.

Each morning, the wood planks are brought to school, erased and covered with a new coat of white chalk; more verses are written on them. When the pupil has made some progress in reading, he laboriously learns how to write. . . .

At an age when the child operates in the concrete, the Koran school imposes on him a purely mechanical, monotonous form of study, in which nothing is likely to arouse his interest. The school thus tends to curb his intellectual and moral activity at the precise moment when they should be developing rapidly.[14]

Hadj Brahim, like many other young Soussi-s, escaped the stultifying effects of the Koran school by launching himself into the hurly-burly of retail trade at the age of nine. But it was at the *timzgida* that he received the only "formal" education he ever had, and his recollections of it are not all disagreeable. "The *timzgida*, monsieur, my childhood . . . it was all very difficult. We were always barefoot, even in winter, and we didn't have much to eat, just vegeta-

---

[14] Nefissa Zerdoumi, *Enfants d'hier: l'éducation de l'enfant en milieu traditionnel algérien* (Paris: Maspéro, 1970), p. 196.

bles, vegetables. None of us will ever forget the terrible drought of 1927. Everybody left the valley just to save themselves. There couldn't have been more than 10 percent of the men who were in the commerce at that time. Everyone was desperate.

"But I always wanted to go to the *timzgida*. When I was a little boy I remember seeing the pupils go off to the *timzgida* every morning, and they would stop at different houses and get little presents, maybe something to eat. And I always wanted to go with them. When I was five I went: every morning from 8:00 to 11:30. We all had our wooden plank for writing [*luha*]. First we learned the alphabet, and then the Koran, verse by verse.

"I always found the punishments handed out to be equitable. After all the *fqih* was fifty-three years at Iskouzrou. He had taught most of our fathers. Everyone knew he was a fair man. He was very respected. There's the old saying that when a father turns his son over to the *fqih* he says 'You slit his throat, and I'll skin him'[15] but that was just a saying. The only time he would beat us was when we used insults. Also, if a student made the same error in writing or reciting three times in a row, he might be beaten.

"I stayed in the *timzgida* four years and I learned the Koran by heart. I still know it by heart. But I never learned Arabic there. It was only later, when I was in the shops in the north and there were no customers, that I learned Arabic. My mother helped a lot. She was literate in Arabic, one of the few, man or woman, in the valley who could read and write. She was the daughter of an *'alim*[16] from Tahala.

"I was raised by my mother along with my two sisters.

[15] Variants: 'You kill him, I will bury him.'

[16] An *'alim* (plural *'vlema*) is one certified at a high level in Islamic studies and jurisprudence.

I had an older brother who was already in trade with my father in Tangier when I was growing up. My father died in 1930 and my mother in 1949.

"It was my mother who found me my wife. That was in 1940. My father had already died ten years earlier. I had already been in the north fifteen years. The way I found my wife was not the way it usually happened; that's because my father had died. Usually it was the father who would suggest a suitable wife to his son, sometimes following the advice of his wife. But the father never made the suggestion directly to his son. An uncle or cousin would do it, telling the son about the merits of such and such a girl. The son would know what was up. He would then try to get a glimpse of the girl. There were little arrangements that could be made. The son would hide in the palm trees near the girl's house, and she might come out to grind the argan nuts while the brothers would pretend not to notice that she was being watched. If the son didn't like what he saw, he could make a counter proposition to his father, but always through his uncle or his cousin. Father and son would then bargain indirectly until they agreed on a choice.

"With me it was my mother who had to play my father's role. As it turned out the girl was from Ait Talib, the rival faction at Iskouzrou. My mother had a woman friend in Ait Talib who was also originally from Tahala, and she told my mother what a wonderful, strong girl my future wife was. The girl had no brothers. It was one of my older cousins, an *anflous*, who was the intermediary between the two families and between my mother and myself. I agreed to the marriage. I came down to the valley from Larache and on April 20, 1940, we were married, and in October I left to go to Tangier. A year later I came back

with 60,000 francs and built our house. She is my only wife.
She's not weak like these younger girls. She's worked in the
fields. She's literate too; my eldest daughter taught her how
to read and write. Best of all she's a good saver and doesn't
waste money like most women do."

I asked Hadj Brahim whether the fact that he had not
married a cousin, an ideal that is upheld in other sectors of
Moroccan society, was unusual for the Ammiln. "Cousin
marriage[17] is a device against strangers. People of the Ida ou
Semlal and the Ida ou Ba'aqil like to marry only their cousins. But we don't do that. Still you often hear talk that you
shouldn't marry in such and such a village, that it will bring
bad luck. The best thing to do is marry in the village like I
did." Brahim's older daughter, however, married outside
Iskouzrou.

"You know today sometimes Soussi girls propose to
their parents whom they would like to marry, and the men
sometimes marry foreigners. This always shocks our wom-
en, it makes them mad and jealous. They say to the father-
in-law, 'So, you're going to be the grandfather of little
Nasrani-s [Christians].' And it's true. There have been
some Germans who have married Swasa. They learn to live
just like us, but it's inevitable—the children become little
Germans. No religion, no language, no tradition. Atheists
just like their mothers. We say in our valley 'Better a
chicken than a partridge—the one won't fly away, the other
flies straight to the mountain.' Another proverb is 'If you're
going to build a house, don't look for stone in the fields of
another tribe.'

"At least our women haven't insisted upon inheriting

[17] Parallel cousin marriage is frequently an *ideal* practice in
agnatic descent systems, but as such it may be violated more often
than honored.

according to the *shari'a*.[18] They could if they wanted to, but it would be very insulting to their family or to the family of their husband. This allows us to maintain our property intact. It isn't as if women received nothing. The bride's dowry—jewelry, clothes, money—is supposed to off-set any inheritance when her father dies. Also the girl's parents receive from the groom's family a bride-price [*sadoq*]. The amount is set according to the custom of the tribe. If she divorces within one or two years of the marriage, the father forms a commission to determine the depreciation of the dowry; but generally only the poor do this. If a woman's husband dies, her brothers-in-law will pay her something representing her share of the inheritance.

"The object, you see, is to keep the family property—the house, the fields, the trees—undivided. This is our customary way ['*urf*] and it is not Islamic, it is not *qadiya*. We have an arrangement known as *tunya*. If a man sells a piece of land for one hundred douros, he doesn't sell it forever, he puts it in hock. Whenever he can raise one hundred douros, it is guaranteed that he can buy back the land. Indivision of property is still pretty much the general practice in the valley. When a man buys back his land the act of his reappropriation is known as the *leftida* [from Arabic, to redeem]. These practices have caused all sorts of problems from the *ulema* because they go against the *shari'a*. But it is believed that if land sales became definitive, no one would come back to the Sous. The way it is, a man can sell in hard times, make some money elsewhere, and come back to the valley to repossess his land."

The childhood memories of Hadj Brahim's children, their vision of their origins and the society from which they

---

[18] The *shari'a* states that daughters or wives are entitled to one-half the share of any male descendants of the deceased.

spring, will differ greatly from those of their father. Living with Brahim in his apartment in Casablanca are his daughter, Najma, eight years old, and his son, Hassan, six. His only other living child is an older daughter, married to a trades-man from the Ammiln, and living at Anameur (one of the first people to have a telephone in the valley, as Hadj Brahim points out proudly). Four other children, born in the early years of his marriage, all died as infants. His first child, a son, died of whooping cough at Casablanca in 1944. During the war it was difficult to get medical attention. A daughter died at Casablanca of rheumatic fever and another son was stillborn. A second daughter died of typhoid. Hassan and Najma now go to Koran school at Casablanca. "They are more like nursery schools than the *timzgidas* in the valley. At least they learn some Arabic. Arabic is the only living language in Morocco[19] and Moroccan Arabic is the closest to the language of the Koran. Egyptian Arabic is incompre-hensible. In any case, we only speak *tashilhit* at home. Berber language will not disappear unless all our sons marry foreigners."

[19] Here, I believe Hadj Brahim means that only Arabic has the vitality peculiar to written languages that are repositories and ve-hicles for true civilization.

Chapter III

━━◆━━

From Tribesmen to Tradesmen

The power of the people of the Sous is lying. All that comes from the Sous is oil, locusts, and a great deal of misinformation.

SONG OF AL-HIBA[1]

Next to the fruit and vegetable sellers, and the sugar and candle merchants, the *baqqalin* from the Sous, retail oil, butter, soft, brown, locally-made soap, honey, fat, and also *kheli'a*—strips of beef, seasoned with salt, cumin, and garlic, then dried in the sun and cooked in large stew pots with fat; a dish that the poor consume in great quantities in the winter."

MAURICE DE PERIGNY[2]

TRADING IN THE NORTH

"I DON'T really know how long people from the Ammiln have been going north for trade, but I don't think it's been too long, probably not more than a century. In any event the Ammiln were the first. As a matter of fact I think my grandfather was one of the first successful grocers. I can't really tell when that might have been. My father died in 1930, and he was around fifty-six years old. So that would

[1] Cited by Col. Justinard, *Le Caïd Goundafi* (Casablanca, 1951), p. 231.

[2] Maurice de Perigny, *Au Maroc: Fès la capitale du Nord* (Paris, 1917), p. 50.

mean that he was born in 1874. He had six brothers, and he
was not the eldest, so maybe my grandfather was born
around 1840. That would mean that he was already in trade
by 1860 and probably made his mark by 1865. His name
was Brahim n'Ait Hussein and people talk about him as
being one of the first. He was a traditional grocer [*baqqal*]
at Fez. [The *baqqal*-s from the Sous generally retailed fat-
based products: cooking oil and grease, clarified butter,
soap, candles.] His clients were all Muslims in the *medina*.
There were no Europeans then; all that came later.

"Of course, men were always leaving the valley. When
there was drought people would flee to the north, over the
mountains to the Haha and the Chiadma, just to see if they
could find something to eat. And then some men began
going to Beni Saf [western Algeria] as miners, but not as
traders—that came later when a few went to Oran as grocers. The miners came back each year with their earnings.
One man walked all the way from Oujda with his miner's
pick on his shoulder so that he could dig a well. That's the
way we are. For the valley, that pick was worth more than
money."

The pioneer emigrants from the Sous must have been
gutsy men. The closing decades of the nineteenth century
in Morocco and the first twelve years of the twentieth were
turbulent, not to say anarchic. The period is known for the
firm rule of Sultan Moulay Hassan, because of his constant
warfare against dissident tribes. It was a period in which
powerful tribal lords dominated the High-Atlas Mountains,
in which Berber and Arab tribes jostled one another on the
coastal plains, in which the cities were vandalized by the
very tribes the Sultan employed to defend them. When
Moulay Hassan died in 1894, the interior situation deterio-
rated rapidly. Numerous pretenders to the throne appeared,

a would-be Sultan swept out of the desert to defend the Muslim community against the impending European onslaught, and, in 1907, the incumbent Sultan, Moulay Abd al-Aziz, was driven off the throne (or from under the parasol, in the Moroccan context) by his own brother, Moulay Abdul-Hafidh. The French, firmly ensconced in Algeria, could not tolerate this turmoil to the west. It was bad for business and besides had attracted the attention of imperial Germany. France reestablished a semblance of order in 1912 when Sultan Abdul-Hafidh agreed to sign a protectorate agreement in order to preserve his own shaky hold on the sultanate.

In the midst of this turmoil, the Swasa began their trek to the north. On foot or on donkey, in groups or alone, they made their way across the mountains to Marrakesh or Mogador, buying, pleading, or cajoling their way through hostile tribes and highway robbers. I once remarked to Brahim how difficult conditions must have been when he first started out in trade in 1925. "Difficult?" he said, "that's nothing compared to the older men, like Hadj Abbid. He used to carry the money of the Ammiln grocers at Tangier back to the valley, alone and on foot, six hundred miles. No roads, but plenty of danger. He is a very tough man.

"Hadj Mokhtar as-Soussi [a famous Soussi historian and theologian whom Hadj Brahim admires greatly] wrote that the grocers of Fez at the time of Moulay Hassan had an *Amin* [a sort of guild head] and this man was himself called Hadj Brahim as-Soussi. He was from Taguenza, not far from Iskouzrou. So by that time there must have been a lot of Swasa at Fez." I asked the Hadj if it was true, as I had read, that Hadj Brahim became a protégé of the French consulate at Fez. "I don't know but it wouldn't surprise me. Everybody wanted to be a protégé in those days. Sultan

Moulay Abdul-Hafidh wanted to impose an obligatory loan on all Moroccan merchants, and everyone wanted to escape it. He called the merchants together, and some claimed to be French and others British, and the Sultan said, 'Strange, for some reason I thought you were Moroccans.'

"In 1907, my grandfather left Fez when Moulay Abdul-Hafidh and Moulay Abd al-Aziz were fighting each other. There was no security at Fez and business was bad, so he went to Tangier, which wasn't in the thick of things. Besides, there were many Europeans there because of the legations. When he reached Tangier, he found a little shop on the *rue de Fes*. The shop was located in a building belonging to a *sharif* from the Tazeroualt by the name of Moulay Ali. He was an acrobat and could speak English because he had been in the circus in America.[3] My grandfather didn't have European clients except for some Spaniards who were as poor as the Moroccans. He was just a *baqqal* as he had been in Fez. I am not sure when he died, but it must have been around 1910.

"I think a lot of Soussi-s began to go to Tangier around that time. As I say, my grandfather had seven sons. He took four with him to Tangier, including my father. Two others were sergeants [*qa'id al-mia*] in the Sultan's army. They were good-for-nothings. The last son went to al-Jadida. He sold skewers of roast meat in the streets there. He married an Arab woman, and no one saw him much after that. Tangier became a big center for the Ammiln at that time. That's where I started off in trade when I was nine years old.[4]

[3] Centuries ago, Sidi Ahmad ou Moussa founded a kingdom in the Tazeroualt region near Tiznit. His descendants are considered *shurfa*. Moreover, he is the patron saint of acrobats in Morocco, and they go to his tomb for blessing.

[4] As of 1903 there was not a single Soussi in grocery trade at Tangier. See G. Salmon, "Le commerce indigène à Tangier," in

"You know, it's rivalry, the spirit of competition, jealousy that pushed so many Soussi-s into trade. Look at my grandfather. People laughed at him at first. Once he came back to the valley for *Id al-Kabir*[5] and he wore fine cloth and *blaghi* [slippers] from Fez. The men snickered at him and he took his children back to the house saying, 'Come, there's no point wasting our time on people who can't appreciate quality.' And one time he came back with the first silver tea set in the valley, and yet another with a good rifle. This was too much for the other men. If he could do it why couldn't they? They had to save face; they were being made to look ridiculous, so off they went. That's the way it still is today."

It was not, then, their awareness of the deteriorating ecological balance that drove the Swasa to the north, but rather the increasingly intense struggle for local prestige.[6] In fact the pecking order in the valley has spurred most of the enterprise exhibited by the Swasa in the past fifty years. This has had numerous repercussions upon the Soussi approach to trade. One grocer from the Ida ou Gnidif, a tribe lying on the northern face of the Jebel Lkist, reported his motto as being "Fill up in the city and empty in the valley. Who knows," he went on, "how long the cities may last. They may be bombed or something. But the valleys will always be there." The Swasa approach commerce as miners. They will mine a vein, their local clientele, until exhausted,

Archives Marocaines, Paris, I (1904), 38–56, esp. pp. 50–51. By the 1930s practically all such trade was in Soussi hands.

[5] The feast commemorating Abraham's slaughtering of the sheep in place of his son.

[6] Cf. Russell Stone, "The Djerbian Ethic: Correlates of the Spirit of Capitalism in Tunisia"; paper presented at the fourth annual meeting of the Middle East Studies Association, Columbus, Ohio, November 6, 1970.

and then move on. There has, until recently, been little attempt to reinvest in their urban businesses, to recirculate their earnings among their clients. Instead these earnings are invested in the valley, not tribally but familially.

In the valley the Soussi can be ostentatious. He occasionally must be, if his local reputation is of any importance to him. In the cities, he is frugal to a fault, a miser in the eyes of his non-Soussi clientele. His penny-pinching is legendary. It is said that if two Soussi brothers run a grocery shop, they share one plate, one bed, and one pair of slippers; for as one sleeps, the other is at the counter; as one eats, the other makes deliveries. A legend which in this case is fact.

Their methods to cut operating costs are myriad, and they will be examined somewhat further on. But all these practices are dropped in the valley. Nowhere is this more obvious than in the building boom among the Ammiln. New and bigger houses are going up everywhere. They symbolize a man's success, and the more visible they are, the better. Often individual houses or family clusters will be built right in the midst of the fields, wasting good agricultural land. The *argan* trees are chopped down, the patiently-built terraces high on the slopes of the mountains are abandoned. Brahim hints at the pressure exerted by his peers that all Soussi-s must feel at some point in their careers. "In that year after my marriage I made good money. An older man from the valley who had a big grocery store at Casablanca offered to let me manage it for a year. With the capital I had, I could have done very well. But I turned down his offer. I had to get back to the valley and build my house. I was twenty-six years old and if I hadn't built that house then, people would have said, 'What's the matter with Brahim? Can't he make it?'"

In the village of Adday there is a big, pink, concrete

villa that dominates the whole *muda*. The house is owned
by three brothers who have been very successful in trade
in Tangier. Their experience reveals a good deal about the
motivations of the pioneers in the north.

They were not the first in their family to go north.
Two older half-brothers, sons of the father's first wife, had
gone to Tangier around the time of the First World War.
These two became the big men of Adday, and the three
half-brothers grew up in their house and in their shadow.
Soon they too were off to Tangier, where the big men
loaned them some money and set them up in their own
business. The young trio soon outclassed their benefactors.
In the early 1920s they moved out of the family home and
built a new one, with a magnificent ornamental door, further up the hill. When the two half-brothers died, they
took over the original house too. In the last decade, over-
coming the suspicions of the villagers, the three brothers
built the big concrete villa. They point out with pride that
they own three houses and do not even bother to use two.

This episode is typical in another way. The older
brothers probably had no illusions about the ambitions of
the three upstarts, yet they had no choice but to set them
up in business. This is what the outsider calls "Soussi solidarity." Then the older brothers simply had to take their
chances in the competition that inevitably ensued. Points
were not scored at Tangier—that is, the brothers were not
trying to drive each other out of business—but the pecking
order of Adday was substantially altered,[7] and that's what
counted.

[7] Adday is another village with two major factions (the Ait
Hsain and the Ait Waqrim) dividing it. It draws its water from
springs across a narrow valley, and today there are two pump houses
and two pipelines that supply the two factions.

Agnates likewise might not treat one another too kindly in the business world. A renowned case is the Mzali brothers who control much of the bus transport in the Sous. They come from the Ait Mzal tribe which, like the Ida ou Gnidif, lies on the north face of the Lkist. Before the coming of the French, the Ait Mzal specialized in camel caravaning, most notably, transporting the annual almond harvest by camel to Mogador. The French had "pacified" their homeland by 1924, and some families made the abrupt, if logical, conversion from caravaning to bus transport. By 1925 they ran the famous "Ait Mzal express," a simple battered bus that bounced over the dirt tracks to Mogador, full of Soussi-s bound for points north. By 1955 the sons of the pioneers in this enterprise—two uncles and two nephews—were operating sixteen buses between Casablanca and the Sous. Twelve buses belonged to the younger Mzalis and four to the elder, and they competed against each other without mercy.[8]

The seed of competition is planted early in the Soussi. Toddlers have their appetites whetted for the adult world and take their first steps into it before they are ten. Among the Ida ou Gnidif this early socialization takes place at the mosque. There, in a separate enclosed yard (*akhourbiche*) where there is a fire to heat the water for ablutions, men who are not in the north gather to prepare tea and to gossip. The little boys join them and listen to the discussions of so-and-so's activities, why X is doing poorly, why Y will soon be rich. The child is thoroughly immersed in the commercial struggle before he ever leaves the valley. Everyone carries in his head a graph of the relative successes, the ups

[8] See André Adam, *Casablanca: Essai sur la transformation de la société marocaine au contact de l'Occident*, 2 vols. (Paris: CNRS, 1968), I, 391.

and downs, of his acquaintances. The graph is subject to constant revision. It is said that when a Soussi comes back to the valley, no one asks "Where have you been?" only "How much did you make?"

Even the pecking order among tribes is subject to revision. The Ammiln today represent the Soussi establishment, but Hadj Brahim indicated that he was aware of challengers among whom a tribe known as the Ida ou Gwagmar figures. "That tribe is doing most of the building in the region these days. They are becoming very prosperous but they are not in trade. Their men go off to work in industries in Europe. They go for long periods of time, and work overtime and never spend any money. With the high wages they are making I wouldn't be surprised if a lot of other Swasa in other tribes started to do the same thing instead of going into the grocery stores. But most of us prefer to be self-employed. We always say that a penny earned in your own business is better than one hundred earned as salary (Frank diyal tijara khayr min miyyat ijara.)"

"In those early days a man had to think fast, and fortunately Swasa are quick-witted. The Jews at Tangier found that out pretty quickly. They controlled most of the wholesale businesses in foodstuffs, and they discovered that they could market their stocks most rapidly through the Swasa. We worked harder and longer than anybody else, and so we sold more. That's why the Jews were happy to have us, and that's how we became successful."

Only the men and boys went north. The women stayed in the valley to look after the fields. There were always men in the valley to look after the women. Before there were good roads, then men in the north might stay away a year. and then come to the valley for a year while an uncle or a brother took over the shop. When good transportation developed, the men would rotate every six months.

"The most common arrangement was for two brothers to go into partnership [*tusherka*]. They would rent a little shop together and split the initial investment in the stock. Somebody already established in trade might lend them the money, or a Jewish wholesaler might advance their initial stock. Then the brothers would split the debt. Once in business they each would pay in half of a permanent capital fund, say one hundred *douros* each. There were never any signed agreements with anybody because everyone was illiterate. All the records were stored in their heads.

"Then they would begin the periods of rotation of a year or six months. The one who stayed in the shop could dip into the common fund to buy more stock. When his period was up, he would pay back the fund without interest and reconstitute the stock at the same total value as at the beginning of the period. Any profits he made over and above this were all his. Today, this system is dying out. Both partners stay permanently in the city. They only go back for holidays. One will specialize in 'interior' services, selling to the customers, and the other will take care of 'exterior' services, buying the stock from the wholesalers.

"In the old days, the period of rotation was very important. For instance it was best to have only one partner [*masherkil*]. If there were four brothers rotating on a six month basis, the total cycle would take twenty-four months. Each brother would be out of work for eighteen months at a time, which is too long. He would have to look for work elsewhere, perhaps manage someone else's shop. The period had to be honored too. That's how my father became a *hajji*, the only one of the seven brothers to make the pilgrimage. My father was in partnership with a brother at Tangier. My father stayed eight months in the shop once, rather than six. His brother demanded an equal amount of time which threw off the cycle. They argued and my father had to figure out what to do with himself for eight months. This was before he was married, so he went to Tunisia where he worked as a guard in a French enterprise. Then he went to Mecca.

"Another way someone could break into trade was as a manager [*agillas*, pl. *igillassen*, in *tashilhit*, i.e., someone who sits in]. This way a man without partners would turn his shop over to someone while he went back to the valley. The manager could run the shop as he saw fit, just as long as he reconstituted the stock when he left. Any profits he made were split fifty-fifty with the owner. This practice is still very common.

"In both systems, the moment of truth came when everyone gathered at the shop at the end of the rotation period to do the accounts. The man coming from the valley checks with the landlord and the wholesalers to make sure that his partner or manager hasn't left any debts. Then they calculate the value of the inventory in the shop according to that day's wholesale prices. They would go through the inventory can by can, match box by match box, calling out the value of each item with a fair number of people watching to make sure no one cheated. Being illiterate and not too good at multiplication, they couldn't write down so many cans of sardines times so many *ryal* for each can. What they did was to calculate everything in chick peas. They would put eight glasses on the shop counter. The first represented *douros*, the second, half-*douros*, the third, quarter-*douros*, the fourth, half-*peseta*, the fifth, *guirsh*, the sixth, *ujhay*,[9] the seventh, *muzuna*, and the eighth, *suldi* [i.e., a *sou*]. The price of each item was called out in terms of these values, and someone would drop a chick pea into the appropriate glass. When they had gone through the entire inventory, all they had to do was add up the chick peas in each glass to know the total value of the stock." Brahim's description leaves little doubt as to why the Soussi proverb states, "We are brothers; but when we do the accounts, we are enemies."

"One of the things a man fears most is that his partner or manager will abuse his shop, squander the fund, or deplete the inventory. When that happens we say 'he ate the shop' [itcha al-mahal]. This doesn't happen too often because a man's reputation is ruined forever. He won't be able to manage another shop or find another partner. That's why we stick to other Swasa in commerce. There are Swasa in every city, and no Soussi can escape his reputation. If he's ruined in one city, he's ruined everywhere. Some try to go to France. The worst Swasa are in trade in France.

"Of course the Swasa who came up as little boys, like myself, really had a head start. We got to know the business early on. We took care of the shop sometimes, made deliveries, kept accounts. Most important we got to know people—future clients and other retailers. We got to know the wholesalers when we picked up goods for the shop. If we could establish a good reputation with the wholesaler then we wouldn't have any trouble obtaining credit or inventory when we opened our own shops.

"At first there was no system as to how you got credit.

[9] From the Arabic word for "face" because this particular coin, apparently from Italy, had a face on it. Brahim is describing the system at Tangier, where there were several kinds of currency in circulation.

If you could be trusted, someone in your family or from your tribe would help you out. There were no set procedures for paying debts either, except that there was no interest. There weren't many Swasa in trade then, and these things could be worked out amiably. After the Second World War all that changed. The Swasa took over much of the good wholesaling business from the Jews, and there were many more of us in the cities then. The wholesalers supplied credit to the newcomers. They began to run chains of retail shops and took on young men from the valley to manage them. A man would go to a wholesaler for the goods he needed, and they would set a time period for repayment. If at the end of the period, he paid off the debt, the wholesaler would advance him a much bigger stock. The time period and the amount became negotiable and depended upon repayment. Again there was no interest charged. In recent years, the wholesalers have begun to require written agreements and collateral for loans.[10]

"We developed all these methods to succeed in commerce. We were and still are the strongest. No one can compete with us. We weren't like the others who want to

[10] For similar sorts of credit arrangements in Indonesia, see Clifford Geertz, *Peddlers and Princes: Social Change and Economic Modernization in Two Indonesian Towns* (University of Chicago Press, 1963), p. 37. I asked Brahim if the Swasa ever had anything like the rotating credit association described by Geertz and Ardener. He found the idea intriguing but stated categorically that the system never existed among the Swasa. See Clifford Geertz, "The Rotating Credit Association: A Middle Rung in Development," *Economic Development and Cultural Change*, (April, 1962), pp. 241–263; Shirley Ardener, "The Comparative Study of Rotating Credit Associations," *Journal of the Royal Anthropological Institute*, XCIV, 2 (1964), 201–229; and Kenneth Little, *West African Urbanization, Voluntary Associations in Social Change* (Cambridge University Press, 1970), pp. 49–56, 164.

make a lot of money and spend it all at once. We made a little bit at a time, but steadily. One problem, before there was security in the country, was to get the money back to the valley. There were people like Hajj Abbid who would take it back for you, but that was risky. The Swasa at Tangier worked out another way. You see, frequently, going and coming from Tangier, we would take a boat from Mogador. Usually it would be a Spanish cattle-carrier or something like that, and we would sleep on deck with all the cattle. At least you wouldn't be robbed on a boat. But if you were coming back with money you had to make your way from Mogador to Tafrawt overland. It was six days on foot or by donkey; ten days by camel caravan because the camels couldn't go where men and donkeys can. It cost money to go with a caravan and it was risky, but it was foolhardy to go alone. So there might be a man bringing down money for his friends, let's say four hundred *douros*. Four hundred *douros* in metal might weigh around thirteen pounds—very hard to carry but very easy to steal. As it turns out there were Jewish traders from the Tazeroualt and Tahala who sold arms, sugar, and jewelry in the mountains, and they came to Mogador to stock up. There were traders from the Ida ou Gnidif too. They didn't want to carry money with them either when they went to the city. So they would borrow the money they needed from the Swasa coming in by boat. Then they would buy the provisions they needed and transport the merchandise to the mountains. As they sold it off, they would pay back the Soussi in his village, for he was there for six months to a year anyway.

"Now we can send our money back by postal money order. Those orders come from all over Morocco and Europe too. The orders are received at the main post office in Tiznit which is a long trip for people up in the mountains. So each tribe designates an agent, and the orders are all sent in his name. He goes down to Tiznit to collect, and then he is responsible for redistributing the money to the families. He receives a little fee from each family for doing this."

Hadj Brahim is old enough to have participated in many of the practices devised during the pioneer years of the Soussi venture in commerce. "In 1925 I went to work for my mother's brother at Tangier. She put me on the donkey that took me over the Lkist to the Ait Mzal. And then I went by donkey to Marrakesh. From there I rode on a wagon to Casablanca, a trip that took three days. Then I took a cargo boat to Tangier, sleeping on the deck with the animals.

"At that time my father was at Iskouzrou. He was very sick from asthma, and he was forced to leave Tangier, where the climate was too difficult. He went to Casablanca and sold charcoal in the Old Medina. He took my two older brothers with him, but when I was ready to go north there was no need for me in Casablanca. That's why I was sent to Tangier. One of my brothers later died of a cerebral hemorrhage and the other now runs a shop for me in Tangier that I turned over to him some years ago. He doesn't know how to write his name, and he never even went to the *timzgida*. My father took him to Casablanca when he was very young. He's sixty-two now. We were all in trade when my father died in 1930. There would always be one of my uncles in the valley to keep an eye on my mother, but she did work the fields. When I married, my wife would help her, and my sisters helped too.

"My mother's brother was a grocer at Tangier, needless to say, because that's what we're known for, grocery trade [*bisri*, a Chleuh version of the French *épicerie*]. My uncle had travelled all over Europe. He took me on as an unpaid shop boy, and I guess we had disputes pretty often. One time I left the shop to work as a shepherd for a Spaniard named Bernardo. I helped deliver milk at Tangier too. He paid well. My uncle came and took me back. He said, 'You may become a Nasrani.' I once worked for an Arab spice seller [*'attar*], a man from the Jebala. We followed the Spanish army through the Rif mountains after the defeat of Abdulkrim.[11] I guess I was around eleven years old then. The Jebli paid me half a *douro* a month. I gave that up and went back to my uncle. Then there was another dispute, and off I went again, this time to herd cattle. I was well fed, but my uncle found me again. A fourth time, in 1929, I just walked off to Arsila hoping I could find work. I arrived and had nothing to eat, so I went to the mosque where someone gave me some food. It was a stupid venture, and I managed to get a ride with some Spaniards back to Tangier.

"About this time I spent the summer in Belgium. There was a Belgian couple at Tangier who were clients of my uncle. They had a son my age, and we were friends. They wanted to adopt me, and I went with them to Belgium to Charles-le-Roi. But I never really planned to stay. I just wanted to look around. I went back to Tangier when I heard that my mother was convinced that I would become a Christian. She wrote me that my father was very ill. My uncle gave me five francs and a bus ticket and I went to Iskouzrou. My father died that same year.

"When I was in the valley I complained to one of my cousins about my work at Tangier, but he just gave me twenty francs. It was my cousin, the *anflous*, who helped me. He contacted a friend in the neighboring tribe

[11] The leader of the famous Rif rebellion of 1922 to 1926.

[Agounsi-wasif] who had a grocery store at Casablanca. He took me on as co-manager of the shop along with his own brother. There I was, seventeen years old and finally beginning to earn some money. The shop was one of the first Soussi groceries to sell to Europeans [*épicerie moderne*]. It was near the municipal swimming pool, and we sold everything—wine, cheese—everything. It was very difficult work. We had some business from the soldiers also, because the barracks were nearby. It was about this time that I really began to learn Arabic, reading everything I could get my hands on during slack periods in the shop. Up to then I used to write my mother and father in *tashilhit* using the Arabic script I had learned at Koran school. At Tangier I had learned how to speak Spanish, and at Casablanca I began to learn French.

"I stayed in that shop from 1930 to 1933, and my brother managed a shop at Tangier. We worked hard and were able to pay off the two hundred *douros* in debts my father left when he died. During 1933, I made my first profits, and I bought some clothes and rugs, and I made some repairs on my father's house. Then I bought a rifle for thirty-five thousand francs. In 1934 the French took it."

Hadj Brahim had purchased his rifle to help defend the valley against the French, and, I suppose, to demonstrate that he was a man. Here was a young Soussi who had had Europeans as clients, who had learned two European languages, and who had almost been adopted by a European family, buying a rifle to do in his erstwhile customers. Sell wine to the soldiers at Casablanca and shoot them in the Sous. His behavior was by no means unique. Thousands of other Swasa, who had worked in Paris during the First World War, or who had European clientele in Moroccan cities, began to drift back to the Sous in 1933 and 1934 to defend their valleys against the French. It was one thing for the French to run the cities, for the French did a good job of protecting the "mines" that the Swasa were working. However, when the French sought to pacify the Sous, where the migrants had invested all their earnings, that was far more threatening.

I doubt, however, that many Swasa were unaware that the French would bring a stability to the mountains that had not existed before; that they would build roads and possibly even schools. Moreover, the remarks of Swasa about this period indicate that they did not resist with any great fervor. They did what they had to do to defend their valleys and their honor, but there were no false heroics, no suicidal resistance in the face of an overwhelming military force. The Swasa, like many other Middle Eastern tribal groups, could fight and trade with their enemies at the same time. The wins and losses incurred in such conflict were regarded as temporary and inconclusive. Power advantages, in the Soussi mind, are seen as inherently unstable; eventually the victor will become the vanquished. Conflict is inevitable, but one should limit the damage by avoiding intransigeance. The Swasa made their stand and lost. They made their peace with the victors, and then, twenty-two years later, helped them pack their bags.

"When the mountains were threatened, we had a system of defense that involved all the tribes. A council of all the tribes would be formed [*amqun*, or what Montagne and Adam translate as *leff*, although in Brahim's sense of the word it has nothing to do with an alliance] with representatives from each. A chief [*amghar*] would be chosen to lead the resistance. This was what happened in 1928 when the French began to move toward the mountains. The

Ammiln organized their first levy [*harka*] of men in that year to fight the French. All the other tribes did the same thing. The *amghar* was a man from the Ida ou Kensous. They were feeling most of the pressure from the French at Taroudant.

"These levies were organized by each *afus*. In 1928 there was what we call a 10 percent *harka*; that is, 10 percent of all eligible men in the *afus* were called up for duty of eight to fifteen days at a time. Men over seventy or boys under eighteen were exempt. So were *tulba* and the crippled. The *anflous* would be responsible for meeting the quota. Depending on the danger, eighty percent of the eligible men might be mobilized.

"In 1933 and 1934 we mobilized at 60 percent. The French were closing in from all sides. The Ait Ba-amrane were boxed in by the Spanish at Ifni and Catroux's troops at Tiznit. Geraud was leading troops up from Tata-Akka, and Martovich moved toward the Lkist from Taroudant.

"Our last stand came in February, 1934. It was on the territory of the Ait Abdullah, and it was terribly cold. The Afelli-wasif were assigned a section of the 'frontier' to defend, and we rotated *harka*-s from our tribe there. I was called up as part of the levy from Iskouzrou. Unfortunately our levy—we were all from the Ait Bilq faction in the village—was assigned a position right alongside a group from Ait Talib. We didn't like this at all, and we complained to the *amqun*. They weren't too happy, and they sent us to the worst place, the *agadir* of Tizi Imili.[12] It was on the top of a promontory where it was extremely cold, and it was an easy target for French artillery. There were eighteen of us from Ait Bilq and twenty men from Agounsi-wasif with whom we got along very well. A few minutes after we

[12] An *agadir* is a communal store-house that is often fortified.

finally abandoned the agadir, it was almost totally destroyed by artillery fire.

"On February 23 the French began to machine gun our positions and to drop bombs. They didn't do any damage, and no one worried about them.[13] Then the French dropped tracts all over the mountains, containing a message from the Sultan asking us to give up in the name of Islam and the 'Alawite throne.[14] I remember that everyone ignored them and began to say that he was just the Sultan of the French. But you know what happened to those tracts? Around 1951, when the nationalist movement was becoming powerful, the French tried to destroy the religious courts of the *shari'a* in the Sous. They wanted to reintroduce Berber customary law just the way they did in the Middle Atlas in 1930. The French were afraid that all our *tulba* would lead us into the nationalist movement, and they were right. We have always had our *shari'a* courts, and we are faithful Muslims. So we sent a delegation to see the Sultan, and we showed him the tracts from 1934 that he had signed. And we said, 'We surrendered in 1934 in the name

[13] When Brahim was telling me this, I was struck by the gaps in experience that have developed among different sectors of Moroccan society in this century. In the north, in the Jebala region, the Spanish had done some bombing a few years earlier in their own pacification program. The rebel chief, Raissouli, reports that his men thought that the airplanes were great birds dropping explosive eggs. But for the Swasa there was no mystery about airplanes. In fact some Swasa may have helped build them during the First World War in France. See Rosita Forbes, *El-Raisuni: The Sultan of the Mountains* (London, 1924), p. 124.

[14] Mohammed bin Youssef became King Mohammed V of independent Morocco in 1956. He died in 1961 and was succeeded by his son, the currently reigning Hassan II. The royal family is known as the 'Alawis.

of Islam and the 'Alawite throne. Now you must defend Islam in the Sous against the French.'

"Well after the tracts came the final offensive. On February 29 we saw thirty-two trucks full of Legionaires, Senegalese, and partisans[15] coming up from the Sous valley. That evening we saw their campfires, and while we were shivering in the *agadir*, they held a big *ahwash* [a regional form of dance about which more later] to try to soften us up. Then on the 30th they attacked after a heavy artillery barrage by the 75mm field pieces. A second column had advanced from Agadir so we were outflanked. The *harka* was broken and we fled between the oncoming columns. The French arrived at Tafrawt even before we were able to straggle back. That's where we surrendered and that's where they took my rifle.

"Everything changed when the French took over, but they did bring security. They appointed their own officials in the villages whom they called *amghar*. Today this same official is called *sheikh* and is appointed by the Ministry of Interior. At Iskouzrou the French appointed a man from the Ait Talib, a known assassin. The Ait Bilq were opposed, and we offered my cousin as *amghar*. All of the tribe of the Afelli-wasif had to choose whom they felt was best, and they settled on my cousin. But that didn't put an end to it because the Ait Talib were angry. There was some fighting, and the French fixed us both and made a man from the Agounsi-wasif *amghar* of our village. Actually that wasn't so bad. We of the Ait Bilq have many friends in the Agounsi-wasif.

"There weren't many problems after 1934 and things

[15] Moroccan tribesmen who fought for the French. Apparently these partisans were from the Arab tribes in the Sous Valley itself.

were pretty calm. You know, some people from the Ammiln were able to profit from the French presence. That was true especially for the people in the tribe of the Ait Tafrawt because they lived near the French administrative head-quarters. The French used them as informants on what was going on in the valley, and in return made sure their busi-nesses were well-protected in the north. That's why the people of the Ait Tafrawt are the most successful trades-men today, particularly the people from the village of Aguerdoudad.

"There were only a few incidents in the mountains after the French came and practically none in the Ammiln. But in the Ait Waqrim [a tribe on the north face of the Lkist] there was a sort of insurrection in 1937. There was a *fqih* [religious teacher] from a tribal fraction known as the Ait Waghzen. This man was a Tidjani,[16] and he had many followers. He kept talking about a miraculous upris-ing against the French, and he used his 'magic' to convince people. He showed armies marching on a sheepskin. The French knew what was going on through their spies. One night the *fqih* led his followers in an attack on a French *caserne*, but they were waiting for him and killed many people. A terrible repression followed in the entire region. Si Brahim, the man who founded the Ait Mzal express, was killed by a rival whom the French supported.

"The first bus between Tafrawt and anywhere started service in 1935, going down to Tiznit. I went back to Casa-blanca that same year. Another man from Iskouzrou went into partnership with me, and we rented a grocery store in the Racine quarter. That didn't last too long because I felt my partner was giving too much credit to the customers.

[16] One of the most powerful religious orders in Islam and cer-tainly in Morocco.

He bought me out, and I went off on my own. Times were bad. The depression was beginning to be felt in Morocco. It was hard to find a shop. I remember walking down the street one day, and I passed in front of this big house with its windows open. I saw that one of rooms was empty, and so I went right up and knocked on the door. The maid called the master of the house, and he came to the door. He was a Fassi. I asked him if he would let me rent the empty room and use it as a shop. He agreed, and I installed myself, enlarging the window and building some shelves. The man turned out to be Si Yaacoubi, and his son, Hassan, later married one of the royal princesses. He used to sit on my counter when he was a little boy.

"Working a shop like that is the same as forced labor. At two in the morning you would go to the big wholesale market for vegetables and fruits. When you arrived there, you might find seven or eight thousand people. You had to be there early before the prices went up and all the good produce was bought: four was too late. Then you had to find someone with a pushcart to take what you bought back to the shop, sometimes clear across town. At six in the morning you would open your shop and at eleven at night you would close. I don't have any idea when we ever slept.

"We were all desperate in those years. There was tremendous inflation and no profits. Many people were out of work and we grocers competed fiercely. We used to go from house to house, knocking on doors, looking for customers. In 1936 we Swasa organized a kind of strike at Casablanca against a Jewish firm. It may have been the first time that there were enough of us around to do that sort of thing. You see, there were these two Jewish brothers who sold household goods. They ran a number of department stores and to encourage their own sales they had stamps.

Now they sold these stamps to retailers who sold their products. The retailers had to give them out free to their clients with their purchases. Then the clients could go turn them in at the department stores for merchandise. Of course these were European clients, and they all demanded these stamps. But we retailers couldn't afford them, so we got together and decided to boycott this outfit and not sell its products. It was a boycott organized by the Swasa and it worked. The two brothers were angry but there wasn't anything they could do. Even the Jewish retailers in the *mellah* [Jewish quarter] joined the boycott.

"I went back to the valley on July 18, 1936. I remember that civil war had broken out in Spain. Finally I contacted someone I knew from the Ait Smayoun who sold clothes at Settat. He gave me his shop as manager, and my brother came down from Tangier to run my little grocery shop at Casablanca. Times were really bad. Nobody had any money to spend. We were practically giving cloth away at Settat, but there were no customers. There was famine in the country, and everything was done by credit. You might see a little money, about once a month. The shop would be open at six in the morning and at eleven you'd still be waiting for the first sale. The *kisra* [native loaf of bread] sold for only fifty *centimes*, but people were dying from hunger. Japanese cloth sold for 1.25 francs the meter, and people were naked. In 1942 when the Allies landed, everything changed. Before there was lots of merchandise and no money; after 1942 there was lots of money and no merchandise.

"In April, 1938, off I went to the valley to see if I could find another shop to manage. The brother of the cousin who had helped me in the past gave me his tobacco shop at Tangier as manager; but that didn't work. A year later I took over another tobacco shop. Tangier began to come to life as war approached in Europe. There were many Polish and Czech refugees. After nine months in that shop I went to Larache to manage a grocery store there. But everyone was miserable there, even the Spanish who lived with their goats. I only stayed four months, and then I went back to Iskouzrou. That's when I was married, April 20, 1940.

"The following October I returned to Tangier for a year. The Spanish had established a sort of military occupation of the city because of the war. The city was cut off from the rest of the country, and it was very difficult to get in and out. However business was very good, and I made sixty thousand francs. The question was how to get the money back to Tafrawt. One had to have a safe conduct pass, and because so many people wanted them, they were difficult to obtain. All the Swasa were in the same boat. But I had this French customer, an officer who went over to the Free French and was living all alone at Tangier. He didn't speak any Spanish, and we became friends because I spoke French. Every night we would listen to the BBC to hear De Gaulle's statements—Churchill too. The officer had some pull with the authorities, and he arranged a safe conduct pass for me. One day I went to the police headquarters with a note from him for the boss there. I showed it to a guard who led me past hundreds of people waiting for their papers. Most were Swasa. Five minutes later I came out of the office with my pass, and all the Swasa began milling around me asking how I did it. 'God is great,' I replied. However I did take money to their families when I went back to the valley.

"There was an older man from the Ait Tafrawt, Amshaw was his name, who had been very successful at Casablanca, one of the first to make it big. He had several grocery stores, and he proposed that I manage the most important one. I had to pass up his offer, for it was high time that I built my house at Iskouzrou. But in October, 1942, I took up his offer and went back to Casablanca. A month later the Allies landed.

"When that happened, business was very good. Everything had been rationed up to then, but the black market was booming, and the Americans had a lot of money to spend. I had mostly military clientele, and I was making sixty thousand francs a month. Now, that was good money!

"The American GI's sold everything they owned and bought anything they saw. You could mix together a little sugar and vinegar and sell it to them as wine.[17] But they sold us their bed sheets. You know the blue fabric that we use all over the Sous for our clothes? Well, because of the war we couldn't get this cloth any more. But the Americans sold us all their sheets, which we dyed blue and used back in the Sous. I'll always remember one evening when four of us were in Amshaw's shop, which was near the port. We were eating a couscous, and an American came in, and we asked him to join us. We didn't speak any English, but he made it understood that if we wanted something, he would get it. Well one of us wanted some flashlights because they were selling very well, so we held up our hands as if holding a flashlight, pushing the switch on and off. He nodded and said 'Okay' and disappeared. About an hour later he reappeared with a huge sack over his shoulder. He laid it on the floor, opened it up, and it was full of pistols!

"Another time I was asleep in my shop and a drunken

[17] At Meknes, the Jews mixed their own powerful date liqueur (*ma-ḥiya* or *eau de vie*) with lemonade and sold it to the GI's as vintage champagne. The Americans bought every bottle they could get their hands on.

soldier came in and woke me up. He had seen the bed and figured my shop was a hotel. I told him it wasn't, but he said 'It's a hotel' and flopped down on my bed. He handed me all the money he had, seven dollars and went fast to sleep. No way to move him because he must have weighed two hundred pounds. About a half hour later, he woke up, looked at me, and said, 'Thank you very much—good hotel' and staggered off into the night."

The war years marked a turning point for the Swasa. The pioneers had fought their way to prominent positions in urban commerce. They were firmly established in grocery trade in several cities, and a number of them had succeeded in becoming wholesalers in foodstuffs. In the preceding decades, food wholesaling had been predominantly in the hands of the Jews, but they gradually ceded their enterprises to Swasa, many of whom they may have supplied in earlier years. The Jews themselves were moving up in the commercial hierarchy and into the liberal professions, so that these transfers were amicable. But the process represents something more important: the development of a power hierarchy in the Soussi communities in the cities. The wholesalers wielded great influence within their own network of relations, helping out tribesmates and setting up younger Swasa in business. All this was on an unprecedented scale because the stream of emigrants from the mountains had become a flood. Among the tribes living on the slopes of the Lkist, few families did not have *at least* one male active in trade in the north.[18]

The growing numbers of migrants posed—and continues to pose—questions of absorption. Fewer and fewer

[18] In 1960, there may have been 7,000 Swasa in retail trades in Casablanca alone. For a good treatment of the magnitude of Soussi emigration, see Noin, *Population rurale*, II, 189–210.

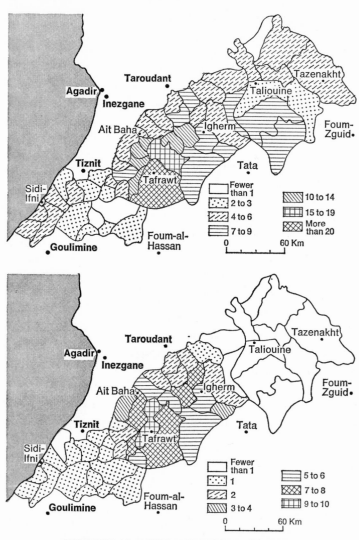

THE RURAL POPULATION OF MOROCCO

Top: Number of departures per one hundred inhabitants (in 1966; internal emigration). *Bottom*: Ratio of merchants per ten temporary emigrants (in 1965; total emigration). (Redrawn by permission from International Bank for Reconstruction and Development, *The Economic Development of Morocco* [Baltimore: Johns Hopkins University Press, 1966], facing p. 6.)

young Swasa could enjoy the privilege of selling to middle class Europeans; more and more established their first businesses in the Muslim quarters, such as the Nouvelle Medina and Derb Ghallef at Casablanca. Hundreds more filtered into the shanty towns. They were staked by the pioneers, by now venerable figures with large amounts of capital. But the influence of these big men was unilateral. Unlike the *anflous*, who was "chosen" and continued in office only through the good will of his lineage mates, the wholesalers owed their power to their acumen in trade. They were only remotely accountable to their tribesmates. Several of them constituted large patronage systems, their protegés being Swasa whom they set up in business. The wards had no ready means to defend themselves against their patrons other than to try to pit one big man against another. The big men, however, have not permitted their commercial rivalries to interfere with their sense of their place at the summit of the emerging hierarchy. An older Soussi whom I had queried about the growing stratification within the community did not deny it. Instead he said, "Look at your hand. Some fingers are longer than others, some fatter, some stronger. Yet all of them work together and do their share without fighting. And that's the way it should be in society."

Some highlights of the career of Hadj Abbid, today almost a legendary figure, may clarify this process. Hadj Abbid, as mentioned earlier, started off as a money carrier in the late nineteenth century. He was born in the *muda* of Addad right next to the market at Tafrawt. At the turn of the century he went to Casablanca and opened up a shop in the Old Medina. It was literally a hole in the wall, a stall built into a rampart of the Medina. He was a *baqqal*, selling cooking oil, soap, candles, and so forth. His shop was not far from the tomb and shrine of Sidi Bilyut. Muslim women would go there for the saint's blessing and leave behind candles in his honor. Hadj Abbid arranged with the man in charge of the shrine (the *muqaddim*) that he would snuff out the candles and bring the remains to the Hadj's shop for a modest fee. The Hadj could then melt them down and make new candles, or sell the butt-ends to the poor.

By 1910, even before the first large influx of French in the city, Hadj Abbid moved out to the Route de Strasbourg, which was to become the major center for Moroccan commerce in the city. He branched out into hardware as well as groceries, supplying himself through Jewish wholesalers. He was already something of a legend in the 1920s, having acquired first a bicycle, next a motorcar, and then, to top it all off, life insurance.

During the depression years, he moved into the wholesale business and in the post-war years ran a chain of retail shops that may have totalled two hundred. He had become wealthy, although it is said that he still wore baggy *siroual* and carried large sums of money in his waistband. Hadj Abbid made credit available to newcomers to the city. He could stock one's shop out of his own warehouses or set one up as a manager in one of his shops. In short, he had become a patron with several hundred clients. His activities broadened, and in 1951 he was elected President of the Moroccan section of the Casablanca Chamber of Commerce and Industry (CCI). He launched himself into light industry, milling (Moulins Ifriqiyya), and cooking oil. He bought good agricultural land outside the Sous, but at the same time built an imposing house at Addad. Now in his eighty's, he has a half-brother who manages his affairs. It is widely believed that he is one of the wealthiest men in Morocco.

There are others like him. Si Hassan, from Aguerdoudad, is known as the King of Tea because of the fortune he made in tea wholesaling at Casablanca. Another Aguerdou-dadi is Oulhaj, now president of an important firm manufacturing petroleum products. Two younger Swasa who have gone far are Si Lahcen of Rabat and Abdullah Souiri,[19] President of the Casablanca Chamber of Commerce. Lahcen started out as a shoeshine boy and then sold vegetables to the American naval base at Kenitra in the early fifties. From there he went into nightclubs for military personnel, and then established several nightclubs and restaurants at Rabat and Agadir. Abdullah Souiri helped his brother selling fried doughnuts in the streets of Essaouira. Today he heads a firm manufacturing dry-cell batteries. These are the men who most conspicuously succeeded in the battle for prestige that, over the decades, drove the Swasa north. And it was in the city of Casablanca, the hub of Morocco's commercial network, that the Swasa registered their most notable successes.

Hadj Brahim brought his wife to Casablanca in 1944 when he acquired a shop in a native quarter known as Derb-al-Kabir. He rented an apartment nearby. That he brought his wife along anticipated a major change in the migration habits of the Swasa: increasingly they brought their wives and children to the city, abandoning the rotation system as they lost interest in their fields and trees.

"I didn't stay long in that shop. My brother-in-law, the husband of my sister, had a shop which I took over as manager. I left my own shop to be managed by a friend. In 1946, we went back to the valley because my wife was pregnant. But I was soon in the north again, this time in a little

[19] Both Lahcen and Souiri are from the Ait Souab and not the Ammiln.

town near Casablanca, Sidi Nasiri. I managed a canteen owned by a French woman, at the railroad station. I stayed there until 1950, the year after my mother died. That year I went back to Casablanca to the Spanish quarter at Ma'arif. For the first time I had a big grocery store; the whole thing cost me 250,000 francs.

"In those years the nationalist movement became very important, and I began to work actively for the Istiqlal party. I helped organize cells in the city. But I was too exposed at Ma'arif, and I turned over my shop to a manager and took an apartment at Derb as-Sultan [part of the Nouvelle Medina]. I brought my brother down from Tangier to manage another one of my shops. At the same time I bought a tobacco shop at Bouchentouf [one of the sprawling new native quarters] where I wouldn't be so visible. I was part of the Istiqlal cell at Bouchentouf, and I spent a lot of my time helping organize the party. On December 8, 1952, I was arrested along with most of the party people after the riots at Casablanca. When I was released, I went back to Ma'arif and took a stall in the public market there. Living right among the Europeans, I wasn't suspected of anything. So I started to help the Istiqlal again, hiding and transferring arms for the urban resistance. I stayed there until 1956 when Morocco finally became independent. Soon after independence, I was rewarded for my services during the nationalist period. The Casablanca representative of the Ministry of Commerce helped me obtain a wholesaling license as well as a franchise to wholesale tea and sugar. Hadj Abbid loaned me money to buy the stock. You know, the depot that I set up then on the Route de Mediouna is the same one I'm in today. I haven't changed much, I am not one of the really important wholesalers. My business provides me a living, and that's all I ask."

OUT-GROUPS: THE FASSI-S AND THE JEWS

The Fassi and the Soussi-s are always after money; they never sleep.[20]

The Swasa did not have to fight their way into urban trade at the expense of other groups. In virtually all Moroccan cities, and certainly Casablanca, they grew with the cities themselves, particularly in the boom years following the Second World War, when French investments generated a new surge of purchasing power in the European and the Moroccan communities. Nevertheless, some group friction developed. The major antagonists were the Jews, the Fassi-s and the French. But the friction among these groups was largely perceptual, and seldom operational. Contact among them was minimal, and thus only limited opportunities arose for one group to trespass upon the territory of another.

The spheres of influence were somewhat as follows. The French controlled most of the industrial enterprises, the banks, and the big importing houses. They favored Jewish entry into import-export, insurance, real estate, and the liberal professions. The rise of the Swasa in food retailing and wholesaling was abetted by the Jews but did not concern the French one way or another. The Fassi-s had established themselves as the masters of the cloth trade in Morocco, handling imports and exports through Casablanca and distribution throughout Morocco. Their status in this respect was confirmed long before the French came to Morocco.[21] However, the Fassi-s were thwarted in their efforts

[20] Edward Westermarck, *Wit and Wisdom in Morocco: A Study of Native Proverbs* (London, 1930), p. 250.

[21] All three groups—Fassi-s, Jews, and Swasa—fulfill in large

to move into other branches of commerce and industry, as major investment capital remained largely in the hands of the French. Each group—the Jews, the Fassi-s and the Swasa —had its own separate fields of action. Only at the summit of the hierarchy of each group would business relations and contacts with another group be established. Soussi big men might go to the banks for credit, something the grocer would not consider.[22] Important members of all three communities might pool resources to import a large shipment of cloth or tea. Any combination of big men could agree to finance a bus line, a textile plant, or a hotel. If something went awry, mutual recriminations might attribute the failure to the alleged cupidity or stupidity of the other group. Then those who see the Moroccan social process in terms of conflict between tightly-organized ethnic, tribal, or religious groups would say, "Aha! the old Soussi-Fassi rivalry again." My own feeling is that such *inter*-group conflicts were no more or less intense than the *intra*-group conflicts mentioned with regard to feuding in the Sous. The difference is that more reliable procedures exist for sanctioning the misconduct of those who share your blood than of those who are outsiders and cannot be held accountable.

During the protectorate years the French remained pretty much above the commercial battle, for they controlled the administration, the banks, and the major industries. However, the Fassi bourgeoisie drew them into the

---

measure the tentative functions of innovative economic leadership in pre-take-off societies, suggested by Geertz, *Peddlers and Princes*, pp. 147–152. See also Chapter VI.

[22] This does not mean that lover-level contacts did not occur. Remember that it was in a Fassi house, that of Si al-Yaacoubi, that Brahim set up his first shop.

fray when they helped finance the nationalist movement in the postwar years. The Fassi-s felt they were being squeezed out of the capital market and denied a fair place in the economic boom. Some Fassi moguls of Casablanca—notably the Sebtis, the Bennanis and the Benjellouns—poured money into the coffers of the Istiqlal party to make it a mass movement. Naturally the French did not take kindly to this tactic, and from 1948 on, there was a running battle between the nationalist bourgeoisie and the French authorities. It culminated in 1953 in the exile of Sultan Mohammed bin Youssef, whom the French judged to be under the thumb of the Istiqlal party and its financiers. Leaving aside this particular period, however, the French were not directly involved in the development of native commerce at Casablanca.

In a physical sense, the Fassi-s, the Jews, and the Swasa all come together on the Route de Strasbourg. Here one finds the cloth bazaars (*kissaria*-s) and warehouses run by Fassi-s, the food and hardware businesses of the Jews, and, since the Second World War, the depots of Soussi wholesalers. The Jews have gradually left the Route de Strasbourg to the Fassi-s and the Swasa. The street terminates in a big square and then continues out the other side toward the Nouvelle Medina, but under a new name, the Route de Mediouna. On one side of the square, the Fassi-s reign; all is cloth, in bolts or finished goods, being loaded on carts or in trucks, fingered by buyers, scrutinized by importers. Now that the Fassi-s are into textile manufacturing in a big way, some of their plants lie close to the Route de Strasbourg, where they maintain their outlets.

On the other side of the square, it is Soussi turf. All is tea, sugar, and cooking oil. The shops are dustier and more battered than on the other side of the square. The turbaned, stubble-faced Swasa in their *siroual*, supervising the loading of wagons for delivery, contrast sharply with the plump, clean-handed Fassi-s in immaculate *jellabas* or business suits, presiding over their cloth a few paces away. The square that separates these two worlds is known as the Place de la Fraternité.

"My business, Monsieur, is mostly with the interior. In fact, practically all the Swasa on the Route de Mediouna sell to wholesalers from the interior. For the city itself, there are wholesalers in each major quarter who supply the grocers there. Now these men, and they're all Swasa too, have a stable clientele because they give credit. Each week the grocer comes in to pick up his stock on credit and the following week, if he needs more supplies, he had better pay off his debt. This kind of relationship can be very stable. But it's not the same for us dealing with the people from the interior. They come into the city to buy supplies, and they go up and down the Route de Mediouna to find the cheapest prices. When the market is stable they don't have much to choose from, but in any case I don't really have what you would call regular customers.

"When the market is unstable, then the brokers [*simsar*, Arabic; *asimsar*, Berber] help arrange the transactions. The brokers used to be all Jews, but there are more and more Arabs who do this now. The brokers move up and down the street checking on the prices. Wholesalers may buy and sell to each other too. For instance, a wholesaler may have to meet a payment and thus unload some stock at low prices. If I have some cash handy I might buy that stock for my own depot. The broker sets up the transaction. If there is an abundance of a certain merchandise on the market, then the seller pays the broker's commission. If there is a shortage, then the buyer pays the commission. The transaction is always anonymous right up until the deal is closed. The broker never says who the two parties are. A broker may never engage in trade himself. That would ruin his reputation and no one could trust him."

When Hadj Brahim talks about Arabs, he has in mind the Arabs from the coastal plains who constitute the bulk of rural migrants to Casablanca. They are distinct, in his way of thinking, from the Fassi-s, although the latter speak Arabic and claim Arab descent. "Now the Arabs were mostly the people from the Chawia (the hinterland of Casablanca). They weren't at all intelligent. On market days they would come to the city to buy a few things and then go back to the countryside. They didn't see their opportunity. For them the city was just a big mystery, and they never tried to find out what it's all about. Now they're beginning to learn. There are a few who are good tradesmen. As for the Fassi-s, they are the bourgeois. They spend more than they should. They don't economize like us. They need good clothes and fancy cars, and they go to the movies all the time. They have made a lot of money in the *kissaria-s*, but they just throw it around. You know the Fassi-s have their own cemetery at Casablanca. The Swasa are buried in the municipal cemetery at Ben M'sik just like everyone else."

The spendthrift ways of the Fassi-s are always subject to Soussi criticism. I remember some Swasa from the Ait Souab telling me with disgust that one of their tribesmates was "no better than a Fassi. He spends his money as fast as he makes it. He had a big Jaguar, fancy clothes, and no one sees him down here any more." What the Swasa resent, it seems to me, is not how much money one spends but where one spends it.[23] The delinquent Soussi just mentioned erred in that he squandered his money in the city—just like the Fassi-s—and not in the Sous. This particular Soussi had "copped out" of the struggle for tribal prestige in order to make his mark in the city. Little by little, other Swasa are following his lead.

Moreover, while it is easy to depict the Soussi-Fassi rivalry in terms of differing life styles and norms, there are factors that join the two groups. One has only to read the descriptions of the spartan *funduq*-s (warehouse-hotel-office all in one) of the bourgeois merchants of Fez, contrasted with the opulence of their private dwellings,[24] to realize that both Soussi-s and Fassi-s are frugal in business without being puritanical in their private lives. The motivations and norms of the two groups may set them apart far less than the difference in scale between the habitual operations in which they engage.

Ghali Berrada recounts a conversation with a Fassi factory owner at Casablanca. The man's conclusions could easily have been those of a Soussi, except that there are few Soussi factory owners. The man in question had originally been a cloth wholesaler and had opened a factory to supply his own outlets.[25]

---

[23] Soussi-s in fact try to live in a Fassi style in their home valleys. Coser has stated this in more theoretic terms: "Out-groups, far from necessarily constituting targets of hostility, can also, under certain conditions, become positive references to the in-group. The out-group may be emulated as well as resented." *The Functions of Social Conflict* (Glencoe: Free Press, 1964), pp. 35–36.

[24] See Henri Gaillard, *Une ville de l'Islam: Fès* (Paris, 1905), p. 158; see also Jerome et Jean Tharaud, *Fès, ou les bourgeois de l'Islam* (Paris, 1930), esp. pp. 44–70.

[25] Ghali Berrada, "L'entrepreneur marocain: Une élite de trans-

Other merchants were interested by my production. That is how, little by little, my factory grew. But so did my commercial problems. Before, I could sell everything I made, whatever the quality.... Today, I have to keep a stock. The stock that you (Berrada) have just seen won't be sold for six months. Competition has made our trade very difficult. We are overwhelmed by taxes. We produce without being sure of markets.... I am really discouraged by this profession, but I can't shut down the factory because everyone will believe that I went bankrupt. All my efforts are aimed at defending my honor and my respected position in society.

While the "smallness" of the Swasa breeds the contempt of the Fassi-s, the latters' "bigness" stirs the resentment of the Swasa. "The problem with the Fassi-s, monsieur, is that they like to dominate. That doesn't sit too well with us, and this rivalry that everyone talks about really began after 1944, in the nationalist movement more than in commerce. The Fassi-s ran the Istiqlal party and made all the decisions. Little people like myself, who helped organize the party, were taken for granted. This situation became much worse after independence when they took over the government. They were the educated ones, the people with money and important friends, and they began to run everything. It was terrible because all they do is find jobs for their relatives and traffic in favors. So I suppose that this rivalry is stronger today than it ever was before. All the same, the Swasa and the Fassi-s get along. You know, the Fassi-s are even using Swasa to manage their cloth shops in the *kissaria*. The Fassi-s that do this will drive their competitors out of business because a Soussi manager is unbeatable."

----

ition." Thèse pour le Doctorat d'Etat en sciences économiques, Université de Bordeaux, 1968, p. 133.

As could be expected, the Fassi-s have their own image of the Soussi, and it is generally disdainful. When one speaks of the Fassi, it is not just any inhabitant of Fez, but rather some thirty or forty illustrious, and sprawling, families that have assured the city its renown over the centuries. The Fassi is a man of breeding, a pacemaker for the rest of Moroccan society. His native city is the center of Islamic culture in Morocco, and he comes from families long associated with great achievements in scholarship and commerce. The Fassi is cosmopolitan. The merchant families, for a number of generations, have established trading colonies in England (at Manchester), Dakar, Marseilles, Genoa, and Cairo. The Fassi is capable of thinking big, of bringing off complicated ventures, and of handling large amounts of money.

When he looks at the Soussi, he sees the inverse of all the qualities he cherishes. He will be the first to tell you about the two Soussi brothers sharing a pair of slippers and a bed. In his eyes, Soussi thrift is miserliness, and the fact that their mother tongue is Berber automatically excludes them from true culture. One Fassi textile manufacturer remarked to me: "The Chleuh? They salt their money away in their socks, if they have any. Some of them make a lot of money, but they don't wear clean clothes, and they don't send their children to school. A Fassi must eat, dress, and live well, educate his children, take his wife to the cinema, have a governess for his children. The Soussi sleeps in the back of his shop, never goes out, eats an onion a day, and makes his children work. The Fassi must start a business capable of sustaining his way of life, and this automatically entails a far greater initial investment than the Soussi. Some of the rich ones still dress like grocers and live in squalid little houses. They never change." I asked him who some of the rich ones are, and he laughed: "Oh, I really don't know their names. You can't remember names like that. They really don't have names. They're all called Ahmad al-Hadj or Hadj bin Ahmad. They're all the same."

It is said that many of the most famous Muslim families of Fez are descended from Jews who converted to Islam in earlier centuries.[26] Under the Merinid Dynasty (1258 to 1465 A.D.) it was decided to house the Jews of Fez in a special quarter—the *mellah*—under the walls of the Sultan's palace. However, many Jews had businesses and homes in the old business district of Fez, and they did not want to jeopardize their interests by moving out. A number of them converted to Islam so as not to be transferred to the *mellah*. But in addition to this interesting piece of Moroccana, the Jewish community of the entire country, some 255,000 strong in 1952, produced several families that rose to commercial prominence in the nineteenth century, particularly at the city of Mogador (today known as Essaouira). There, they pioneered in importing tea and exporting the raw produce of southern Morocco. As the Fassi cloth merchants struck up lasting arrangements with the textile merchants of Manchester, so too the Jewish tea importers entered into intimate relations with the major British tea exporters.

Over the centuries, one could glean evidence for just about any theory concerning the status of Jews in Muslim Morocco. What is essential to an understanding of their status is their dependence upon the protection of someone from the majority community. But that did not mean that they were powerless themselves. For instance, it was generally a Jew who acted as business agent for the Sultan (*tajir*

[26] See Roger Le Tourneau, *Fès avant le Protectorat* (Casablanca 1949) p. 451.

as-Sultan). On the other hand, the Jews could be and often were subjected to Muslim derision and scorn, and occasionally violence. Two anecdotes may give an idea of the relations that might exist between Muslim and Jew.

Chenier wrote as a direct observer of seventeenth century Morocco. In periods of drought, he noted[27]

> The Muslim would pray to God for rain. The children importune the Almighty, and then comes the turn of the *tulba* and saints. Should all these efforts fail, they at last drive out the Jews of the town, and forbid them to return without rain—for, say they, though God will not grant rain to our prayers, He will to those of the Jews to rid Himself of their importunity and the stinking odour of their breath and feet.

A Jewish acquaintance at Casablanca related a story to me of a different nature, about his father who imported tea and bought skins and grain for export. One year, as was his practice, his father made credit advances to several of his Muslim suppliers, to be paid back when the harvest was sold. That year there was virtually no harvest due to lack of rain, and the father simply wrote off all the debts. At one point he went to Meknes and took his son with him. They were invited to dine at the house of an important Muslim notable who had been advanced a particularly large sum of money which he could not pay back. As they ate, the father noticed that it was the Muslim's son who was waiting on table. The father asked his host, "But Hadj, have you no servants to wait on table?" "I have tens of servants," replied the notable, "but I have made my son serve you personally that he may realize the depths to which we would have fallen had it not been for your generosity."

[27] L. Chenier, *The Present State of the Empire of Morocco*, 2 vols. (New York: Johnson Reprint, 1967) I, 346.

With the growth of Casablanca as a major port after the turn of the century, several Jewish families established themselves there. They were active in all the commercial undertakings in the growing city. They rode the crest of the early real estate boom, buying up choice pieces of property in what was to become downtown Casablanca, as well as the area later to be developed as a native city (the Nouvelle Medina). Others bought up pasture land in what was to become the luxurious European residential district of Anfa-Ain Diab. Another group of Jewish families (Nahon, Benchimol, Pariente) innovated in banking, first in Tangier but by 1920 in all Moroccan cities, including Fez.[28]

But it was tea importation that continued to be their special preserve. Until 1958, when the state established an office to handle all such imports, this trade was in the hands of four or five Jewish families: the Toledanos, the Toledano-Pintos, the Amsellags, and the Benazzerafs. Morocco is a nation of tea-drinkers, and importing and distributing this precious substance brought the Jews and the Swasa together.

THE SOUSSI ESTABLISHMENT

The sugar cone in its blue robe, carried on the backs of camels,
There is no pleasure if it is lacking. The snowy sugar, how
    beautiful it is.
The tea of London has beauty and goodness
The tea jar is the minaret of the mosque
The kettle is the *mu'azzin*[29] of course, just along side
And the tea pot is the *imam*.[30] That too is obvious.
The glasses are the rows of Muslims in prayer

[28] See Abdelouahab Lahlou, "Notes sur la banque et les moyens d'échanges commerciaux à Fès avant le Protectorat," *Hespéris*, XXIV (1937) 223–232, 3rd. trim.

[29] He who calls to prayer from the minaret.

[30] He who leads the prayer in the mosque.

And the tea tray is the praying-ground (*m'salla*)
But as for the tea, make no mistake
The Christian, he who knows well that you are his enemies,
He strikes you with his cannons loaded with charges of tea
He ambushes you with his scales
The enemy strikes you in the stomach
The Christian strikes. He aims well. He brings the sugar cone.
If it were good for you, he would not bring anything.

(Soussi poem from the Ait Ba'amrane)[31]

Moroccans annually consume about fourteen thousand tons of green tea imported from the Far East. The British brought the Moroccans into the tea-drinking world not too long after their own conversion.[32] Over the decades, tea has become a necessity in the diets of even the poorest Moroccans. It is a liquid vehicle for the impressive quantities of sugar consumed each year: seventy-seven pounds per capita per annum.[33] The sugar in turn is a major indicator of the malnutrition of much of the Moroccan population. The boiling-hot glasses of mint tea help kill hunger and provide enough energy so that an adult can go about his work. Tea and sugar are thus vital to Moroccans, and they could pass them up about as easily as a heavy smoker his cigarettes. The Soussi poem written fifty years ago was perceptive. Long after the Christians left Morocco, their weapons still strike Moroccan stomachs. Of course, tea and sugar consumption is only symptomatic of underlying economic ills, but Soussi wisdom warned from the outset that these pleasurable com-

[31] From Col. Justinard, "Les Ait Ba'amrane," *Villes et tribus du Maroc*, XIII, 63–66.
[32] See J.-L. Miège, "Origine et devéloppement de la consommation du thé au Maroc," *Bulletin Economique et Social du Maroc*, XX, 71 (1956), 377–398.
[33] "Les industries alimentaires," *La Vie Economique* (numéro spécial, December, 1967), p. 7.

modities must disguise some evil effects. Nonetheless, the Swasa are at home in ambivalent situations, and they were soon past masters in handling the Christians' weapons.

A grocery store could have a great variety of goods, but if there were no tea or sugar, the grocer might not have any customers. He would have to make sure that his wholesaler could supply him with tea and sugar, and not every wholesaler could do that. The wholesaler, for his part, would have to establish reliable relations with tea importers who could supply him. A working relationship between the Swasa and the Jews developed precisely to this end. The Jews found that the Swasa could guarantee distribution of large quantities of tea at low cost throughout Morocco. As the Jews consolidated their position in tea imports, they helped the Swasa consolidate their position in tea wholesaling and retailing. As for sugar, the most popular kind was and is refined locally by a French firm, the Compagnie Sucrière Marocaine (COSUMA).[34] The sugar wrapped in the famous blue paper of COSUMA was what every grocer wanted on his shelves. However, COSUMA supplied only a certain number of franchised wholesalers with its product. Hadj Brahim obtained such a franchise in 1956. In short, Jewish tea importers and French sugar manufacturers fostered the rise of the Soussi big men in the postwar years. The most powerful patrons among the Soussi wholesalers at Casablanca were those men—like Hadj Abbid and Si Hassan—who could guarantee their protegés among the grocers adequate supplies of tea and sugar. Some Fassi-s and Jews prospered in tea and sugar wholesaling also, but by 1958, when the whole system was abruptly changed, the Swasa had the lion's share.

Casablanca was shaken in 1958 by the "Toledano crash." The Toledano Brothers were one of the major tea importing

[34] In 1967, the state took a majority interest in this firm.

houses. Every year, each of the major houses would arrange advances on the tea to be imported for that year from China, Formosa, or Japan. The credit advances involved virtually the entire merchant community of the city—Fassi cloth merchants, Soussi wholesalers, French banks, and so forth. The system worked pretty well, and 15,000 tons of tea were imported into Morocco in 1956, a record that has never been equalled since. In 1958, the Toledano Brothers wanted to bring off another big shipment and set to work lining up creditors for the purchase. As Hadj Brahim recalls, "Everyone was in on it. They passed out promissory notes good for 60 or 120 days against the sums advanced to them. They raised 800 million francs (about $1,600,000) from a hundred or so merchants, and then with that money they borrowed about the same sum from eight banks. The tea shipments never came through, and the brothers were declared bankrupt. I don't know if they made off with the money or what, but I think they're in France now doing pretty well for themselves. I lost a lot of money in that affair."

The Toledano crash decided the state to nationalize tea imports to put an end to tea speculation. A national tea office was set up, effectively terminating the role of the Jewish tea importers. But the creation of the office opened up all sorts of new opportunities to the Swasa, which, with their habitual aplomb, they immediately seized.

The concept underlying the National Tea Office was fairly simple. It was to be a device by which the state could control every stage of the distribution of tea, right down to the final sale in the grocery store. All this was to be carried out at the lowest possible cost to the state, which would directly involve itself with only two phases of the operation: the purchase and importation of tea from abroad, and the packaging of the tea according to various qualities (Chun

Mee, Gunpowder, etc.) consumed in Morocco. Actual distribution would be handled by franchised wholesalers who could supply retailers at prices fixed by the state.

Sixteen qualities of tea are consumed in Morocco, and popular preferences vary from region to region and season to season. In the past there had been widespread speculation on the part of the wholesalers, who would hold a certain quality off the market, driving its price up, and then unload at high profits. The National Tea Office was supposed to put an end to this by keeping large stocks of each quality in its warehouses. If prices were artificially driven up somewhere, then the tea office could flood that particular market with the quality in demand, thus forcing the price back down. Unfortunately, ever since the office was created, it has not succeeded in building up large reserves. In fact, it has imported less tea annually than was the practice before its creation. One reason is that the National Tea Office deals in an imported commodity, so the state has not always provided it adequate funds in hard currency to meet its needs. Second, bureaucrats are probably not terribly adept in dealing with the complexities of international and national markets. Whatever the explanation, speculation and the black market came into full play soon after the establishment of the office, and the Swasa big men became the masters of the new system.

Among the first people to receive franchises from the tea office were the former importers themselves. This was their compensation for the elimination of their profession. Franchises were also granted to a number of wholesalers who were experienced in tea distribution. The total number of merchants who received franchises in 1959 was 137. The group was divided up into five classes acording to the volume of business. A merchant who found himself in Class I would be entitled each month to 7.3 tons of tea of all the qualities available. Someone in Class II would be entitled to 20 percent less and so forth. Hadj Brahim, one of the privileged 137, was placed in Class III, but a fair number of his Soussi colleagues were Class I distributors.

Between 1959 and 1966 the original 137 franchises grew to about 1,200. The franchises had become an integral part of the Moroccan patronage system, like any other officially issued permit or license. Many who received franchises were legitimate tea dealers, but many, many others were acquainted with tea only through having drunk it. Automobile dealers, and policemen, gas station owners and orange growers became bona fide tea distributors. Not having any great interest or expertise in this particular profession, they sold off their monthly delivery slips to full-time distributors. As it turned out, about ten Soussi big men at Casablanca consistently offered the most attractive prices for these slips. Month after month they were able to take possession of quantities of tea far in excess of the amounts to which their own franchises entitled them. In 1967 when the reserves of the tea office were particularly low,[35] these men appeared to have cornered the market.

The Soussi tea moguls (*les rois du thé*, as they are known in Casablanca) controlled enough tea to be able to influence the pricing system dramatically—and, lacking the necessary

[35] Three explanations are advanced for the penury of tea in 1967. (1) The Suez Canal was closed after the June War. (2) An oversight in the 1967 budget practically omitted tea imports. (3) The People's Republic of China, which supplies 60 per cent of Morocco's tea, was irked to learn that debased mixtures of its tea were being packaged by the Tea Office under labels for the finest quality Chinese tea: Chun Mee (Five Stars). A variant is that the debasing was done with Russian tea, which the Chinese found highly insulting. In fact in 1969, the Moroccans concluded a big deal with the USSR to import Georgian tea. Hadj Brahim considers Russian tea "undrinkable."

reserves, there was nothing the tea office could do about it. The moguls manipulated markets throughout Morocco, and as prices soared in one locale they would dispatch trucks of tea to their local distributors. At one point tea could *only* be purchased behind the counter at prices five times the official ceiling. Whatever the ethics involved, one cannot help but admire the ease with which these Swasa grasped the complexities and opportunities of the national market, and the rapidity with which they put their knowledge to good use. In all fairness, some of the glory or opprobrium that such dexterity elicits must be shared by a few Fassi-s who were in on the system too.

Hadj Brahim was not in on it in any big way, but I am confident that he would find the above remarks a fair resume of what happened to the Moroccan tea trade. However, he was in on another aspect of the activities of the tea office: he was at one time an official advisor to the office, participating in official delegations to tea exporting countries and advising on the quantities and qualities to be purchased. Three or four other Swasa served as advisors too, in addition to a Fassi and a Jew from one of the families that had been major tea importers. It is said that even as regards the importation of tea, the tea office allowed itself to be had.

In the years before the creation of the office, the private importers might purchase six or seven thousand tons of tea from Formosa each year. Many Moroccan tea dealers got to know Formosan tea dealers, and even after the nationalization of tea imports, some of the advisors could strongly recommend importing such and such a quality from such and such a Formosan exporter, at a price, obviously, somewhat above the market value, and with part of the Formosan's profit finding its way back to his Moroccan advocate.

At least in the first decade of its existence, the tea office had been victimized by the very people it was designed to control. It seems that one day the advisory council met with the staff and director of the office, and as the afternoon droned on in a discussion of bureaucratic procedure and the shortage of hard currency, the old sharks grew restive. Finally, a former importer shouted across the table at a former associate, "What do you say, Si Abdullah; just you and me. We'll roll in 17,000 tons just like the old days!" The other advisors laughed in approval while the director looked distinctly ill at ease.

Not only did the Swasa big men make their mark in Casablanca in the 1950s and 1960s but so did the Soussi community as a whole. By 1960 there may have been seven or eight thousand Soussi tradesmen in the city, not to mention those employed as workers or in other professions. With the growth in numbers came a growing commitment to the city as well as a growing distance from the Sous. The men now brought their families to the city and put their children in school. Trips back to the valley became less and less frequent, and some tradesmen stayed away years at a time. For the older generation the drive to assert oneself in the pecking order of the tribes began to weaken, and for the young the city became the predominant frame of reference. The Swasa now seem prepared to be judged on the city's terms, and by outsiders at that. They wish to be seen as modern and dynamic. It matters to them what the Fassi, the Jew, the European, the American thinks of their activities.

The growing preoccupation of the Swasa with the city was vividly represented to me on Throne Day, March 3, 1970. For a number of years now, the Soussi community has taken over the Municipal Theatre of Casablanca to put on a marathon performance of Soussi dancing and singing. Throughout the city groups organize celebrations of one kind or another in tribute to the king and his dynasty. But Hadj Brahim told me with considerable pride, "Ours is the best, and everyone comes to it—you must come too."

I did, arriving at around 4:00 P.M. There was Hadj Brahim in white linen jellaba with hood, along with several colleagues, all of whom acted as ushers for the in-coming guests. The Hadj hustled me into the hall packed with a thousand or so spectators and sat me down in a chair of honor. Then off he went to greet other guests, find them good seats, make sure that they were served tea and cookies. He was in his element, moving at a frenetic pace until midnight, although I left long before. He ushered in the governor of the city, the French director of a big Casablanca bank, Fassi textile manufacturers, in fact everybody who is anybody in Casablanca.

On stage we witnessed performances of *ahwash*, a dance form unique to the Sous. It generally consists of a number of women dancing and singing with men accompanying them with tambourines (*adloun*), one-stringed violins (*rbab*), a sort of banjo (*lantar*), and a piece of metal (*naqus*) which is beaten in rhythm. One man (the *rais*) will sing verses, sometimes improvised, while the dancers chant in chorus. André Adam cites one performance of *ahwash* that he witnessed as an example of Soussi prudery vis à vis the behavior of women. The female dancers that he saw performed veiled with their back to the audience.[36]

What I saw was considerably different. There were seven women and four musicians. The women were unveiled, bare-armed, and heavily bejeweled. They wore long green *kaftan*-like garments with gold embroidery. The girls were good looking, somewhat hefty but graceful. Their hair was raven black, braided and piled high on their heads. The

[36] André Adam, "La maison et le village," *op. cit.*

dance that they throw themselves into for fifteen minutes at a time, and with obvious enthusiasm, defies my powers of description. It is a sexy, provocative form of belly dance, all the more remarkable for the amount of clothing and jewelry they wear. There is not the slightest inhibition in any of their movements nor in the reactions of the audience. I remarked to a Soussi acquaintaince that I was surprised at this libertinism, so different from the Calvinist image that is usually applied to the Swasa. "Oh, all that is finished," he replied. "We are modern now, and this is the city."

The vast majority of the spectators were Soussi-s, and they brought their wives and children to see the spectacle. Everyone appeared to enjoy it immensely. A one-legged male singer convulsed the audience with tales of the tribulations of the married man. A Soussi next to me tried to translate but could not stop laughing. The dancers chanted in a peculiarly high-pitched key that in this context was highly sensual. The audience roared its approval. The little old man playing the violin, a veritable Soussi leprechaun, leapt and turned among the dancers, urging them on. And so it went for nine or ten hours, in fifteen-minute sets with ten minutes rest. The hall half-emptied every hour or so and then refilled with new spectators. In this way Casablanca paid tribute to the Swasa. Hadj Brahim beamed as he scurried about.

Chapter IV

———◆◆◆———

Facets of the
Soussi Business Ethic

AN IMAGE OF THE TRADESMAN IN MOROCCAN SOCIETY

He who lacks the audacity to stand up boldly for his
rights, or who lacks the protection of the influential
with respect to the system of justice, it is advisable that
he abstain from commerce, for he will expose himself
to ruin and the loss of his goods; he will, in a way, be
devoured by the other merchants and will fail to see
the law applied to them. So it is that most often people
are covetous of that possessed by others, and in the absence of public authority no one can be assured of con-
serving what he possesses. That is true in particular
for the merchants of the poor, the merchants of the
rabble. . . .

One must have a wily character, skillful and boast-
ful. One must know how to struggle bitterly whenever there is a conflict, to struggle querulously and
stubbornly. Thus is this profession; but these aptitudes
are harmful to one's integrity and virility—they corrupt one's soul.

IBN KHALDOUN (1332–1406 A.D.)[1]

THE OPPROBRIUM that Ibn Khaldoun attaches to those
who engage in trade is not widely shared in Morocco, nor

[1] From G. H. Bousquet, *Ibn Khaldoun: Les Textes sociologiques et économiques de la Muqaddima* (Paris, 1965), pp. 128–129.

in the rest of the Middle East. After all, the Prophet himself was a merchant, and he was not known to have denigrated his past. The Swasa have thus thrown themselves into a profession that is entirely legitimate and respected. Trading is not seen as harmful to one's soul. If this were not the case, it might be tempting to see the Swasa traders as members of a minority or "marginal group" asserting their social worth and seeking status by perfecting their skills in a profession that the rest of society avoids and demeans. Such an explanation might be useful in understanding the development of banking and financial skills among the Jews of Europe and the Middle East, but it tells us little about the Swasa.

Nor are the Swasa members of some schismatic religious sect, such as the original Calvinists, or, closer to contemporary Morocco in time and distance, the Mzabi-s of Algeria and the Djerbians of Tunisia. Such groups, E. E. Hagen has argued, have undergone a process of "status deprivation" within the societies from which they spring, and have, over time, sublimated their frustrations in an intense, individualistic drive for self-realization, generally in entrepreneurial activities.[2] The Swasa, by contrast, are orthodox Sunni Muslims and proud of the fact. Spiritually and ritually, they are in the mainstream of the Islamic community. The entrepreneurial zeal they manifest is not a product of frustration, but rather a reflection of their belief that they can promote themselves upwards as an integral part of Moroccan society.

In writing of the forbidding commercial arena of the fourteenth century, and the character traits necessary for

[2] E. E. Hagen, *On the Theory of Social Change* (Dorsey Press, 1962), esp. Chapter 9. On the Mzabis, see E. A. Alport, "The Mzab," *Journal of the Royal Anthropological Institute*, LXXXIV (1954), 34-44. On the Djerbians, see Stone, "The Djerbian Ethic" throughout.

survival in it, Ibn Khaldoun touches upon factors that are still relevant today. The "merchants of the rabble," of which the Swasa are latter-day descendants, must rely on cunning and courage to make their way among the covetous and predatory big men of the marketplace. But all the cleverness in the world may be of no avail if the tradesmen lack the "protection of the influential" that alone can shield them from the greed of rivals and the arbitrary impositions of the state.

The situation that prompted Ibn Khaldoun's caveat has persisted in important ways up to the present time. In yet other ways, the situation has worsened in the twentieth century: trade has become a safety valve for the increasing numbers of unemployed, a self-initiated and potentially remunerative line of work that can be adopted if one has something —virtually anything—to sell or trade.

The Soussi tradesman finds himself functioning within an increasingly vast sector of Moroccan society that scavenges for survival in professions that can pay off only through extraordinary ingenuity and patience. Hundreds of thousands of adult Moroccans engage in desperate, marginal commercial activities, competing with one another for a smell, if not a taste, of the oil in the rag. The Soussi venture in petty trade had its initial impact in rendering existence in the home valleys a little less problematic. But now the Soussi is fighting for survival in cities where there are too many sellers, and where the buyers are numerous, penniless, and threatening. He is often pitted against a government which could easily break him, yet forced to overcome his innate suspicions and to collaborate with the powers that be in the interests of his own survival. As a "merchant of the rabble" he is frequently in the uncomfortable position of "exploiting" clients who are only slightly more vulnerable than himself. The various balancing acts he must perform vis à vis the government, his clients, and other tradesmen, make a virtue of the craftiness that Ibn Khaldoun deplores. If poor Moroccans resent Soussi tradesmen, it is not for their practices but for the skill with which they carry them out.

There is a folk figure known in all the Arab countries as Juha, or, in Morocco, as J'ha. He is a man of a thousand faces, solemn and mocking, deceiving the unwary by his ostensible naiveté, but also undoing himself by the subtlety of his own pranks. He is forever pulling off an exploit but is never capable of holding the advantage. J'ha continually climbs up out of the rabble, dupes the mighty, and then tumbles back down. Through J'ha Moroccans can laugh at themselves. He makes palatable the machinations that poor men must use to get along in the world and serves as a reminder that successes are at best temporary. Katib Yacine, the Algerian playwright, has described J'ha in terms that I feel are worth repeating, for his J'ha is the embodiment of the values of survival—values which in some respects sustain the relations of petty tradesmen with their clientele: [3]

> J'ha is an intellectual of the people, always involved with their daily concerns. He is a sort of Charlie Chaplin permanently confronting the forces that would crush him, always falling down, getting up each time, and, ultimately, having the last word. And it is in exactly that sense—like Charlie Chaplin—that J'ha is a popular hero. He is at grips with the same problems as the people, he confronts the same enemies, he undergoes the same defeats, and he shares the final triumph with them. By the very nature of things, he is weak at the start, unarmed, and thus obliged to resort to ruse and evasion. Compromise, tactical, temporary compromise, is his indispensable stratagem, his *ruse de guerre*.

[3] Katib Yacine interview in *Mars* (Rabat) n.d. (1968?).

I would add that J'ha is not a positive hero. His personality is not clear-cut. He discovers, bit by bit, the mechanisms of oppression and mystification, as well as the means to overcome them. He is a man of flesh and blood and not an idea disincarnate. He never read Marx! It is through each step of his life—and necessarily through some false steps—that he learns the truth and tests his force and that of others like him. . . .

It is true that at times it seems that J'ha is opposed to the people. In fact there sometimes is a game of competition between J'ha and the people, but what should be noted is that there is no *contradiction* (K.Y.) between the two antagonists. J'ha must be seen as one detached from the avant garde of the people. He is the people put to the test before the Sultan, the Mufty, etc. He incarnates the popular awareness as it emerges, the conscience of the people in action. He is the popular experience with its ups and downs, its defeats and victories.

In his struggle with the powers that be, J'ha dirties his hands, he collaborates with those powers, and sometimes gives the impression of having gone over to the other side. At any given moment, he might seem to be part of the enemy's system. Indeed, because J'ha combats the powers in earnest—and not as a Pharisee—he leaves fingerprints.

David McClelland has argued that in any society it is such folk figures who often reflect the true cultural norms of human behavior. If these figures demonstrate that cunning and sleight of hand pay, then that society will be hard put to develop the devotion to hard work and planned enterprise that ensures economic success.[4] But J'ha does not glorify the methods he practices, for they do not ensure his own success. His experience simply poses the question,

[4] David McClelland, *The Achieving Society*, paperback ed., (Glencoe: Free Press, 1967), pp. 67–70.

"What other methods are there, given the circumstances?" The Soussi, as the remarks of Hadj Brahim bear out, combines, Levantine unscrupulousness with Calvinistic devotion to the task, without ever expecting lasting success.

Two J'ha stories may give a taste of his operating procedures. In the first, it is J'ha revealing the powerful and the reverend for the buffoons they are. Herein, we find him scoring points for the rabble.

> A group of *ulema* came to J'ha one day and said to him: "We have been told that you possess magic seeds that give you your intelligence."
>
> J'ha replied: "Well, I didn't want to talk about it, but it is true. I have such seeds."
>
> "Can we obtain some?" asked the *ulema*.
>
> J'ha pondered a moment: "Yes, that can be arranged, but of course they do not come cheaply."
>
> "How much?" queried the *ulema*.
>
> "1,000 ryal each."
>
> "That is a lot of money," said one of the group, "but I will buy at least one." He gave J'ha 1,000 ryal and J'ha handed him a little seed which the man popped in his mouth, chewed, and swallowed. Then he erupted in anger and shouted at J'ha: "But that's nothing but a pumpkin seed!"
>
> "See!" said J'ha, "you've eaten only one seed and already you're beginning to learn."

So it is that the Swasa, through displays of respect for the authorities, have often taken the government for a ride, an honorable practice in which the rabble can vicariously participate.

In the second story, J'ha turns on the people who sought to profit from the plight of a dying man. Indeed, a recurrent theme of J'ha stories is that the poor are not necessarily pure in heart.

In an impoverished village, there was an old man whose only possession was a donkey whose coat was soft as velvet. One day the old man, whose name was J'ha, became gravely ill and feared that he would die.

He called his neighbors, all as poor as himself, and begged them to pray for him. "If I am cured," he said, "I will sell my donkey and divide the money among you."

All the villagers were excited by the prospect of this possible wealth and began to pray in earnest, day and night. And J'ha was cured. He was also disgruntled by his promise. He thought for a while and came up with a solution.

Off he went to the market with his donkey. Once there he shouted "Who wants to buy my donkey for a *dirham* and my stick for 500 *dirhams*?" Despite the unusual offer many people were attracted by the donkey selling for only one *dirham*. J'ha said, "I will only sell the donkey with the stick." Finally one man decided that even for 501 *dirhams*, the donkey was well worth it. So the deal was concluded.

Then J'ha went to his village where all the people came to greet him and to receive their shares. "My poor friends," J'ha said sadly, "I have nothing to give you. I sold my donkey but I have only this for you," and he threw them one *dirham*. The villagers were furious and protested. J'ha cried out, "May the peace be upon you! Know that the donkey was sold for one *dirham*. I promised you this price and I keep my promise. As for the rest, it is not yours; it is the price of the stick."

The people have been had, but they curse their own stupidity rather than the man who had them. One's individual cleverness and the gullibility of those around him define

what is or is not permissible. In the following pages we shall
see the Swasa reenacting J'ha's role as champion-cum-ex-
ploiter of the rabble. The tradesmen are resented for their
hard, occasionally underhanded, business practices, but respected as examples of the heights to which "little people"
can aspire.

THE UNEASY FIT OF NORMS AND PRACTICES

To hear Hadj Brahim analyze business practices and
what he feels makes for commercial success, one can easily
see in him all the attitudes associated with the Protestant
ethic. David McClelland has laicized Max Weber's original
hypothesis of the interrelation of entrepreneurship and Protestantism by positing that individuals develop a cluster of irrational drives that impel them to achieve, placing them in
constant competition against their own standards of excellence. Hadj Brahim's discussions of his personal ambitions
occasionally fit McClelland's description of the "high need-
achiever." The Hadj in word and in deed is an advocate of
hard work and expertise, of frugality and planning, of individual effort and self-reliance, of clean living and piety.
He sets himself goals. Yet at times, in word and deed, he vio-
lates every one of these norms. Just when one becomes convinced that Brahim is a North African Ben Franklin, he
abruptly becomes the Muslim fatalist, or a grocery store
J'ha taking his customers or the government for a ride. His
personal standards of excellence are momentarily forgotten
as he competes for the recognition of other tradesmen and
tribesmates. A major element in Hadj Brahim's approach to
his profession is his religion. However, the manner in which
he interprets the impact of the hereafter upon his activities as
a mortal will be saved for a later chapter. For the moment I

shall concentrate on his appreciation of the rules and norms of commerce.

"When I was young, I was never two minutes without work; I had a love for this profession. I'd always be about the shop, cleaning the merchandise, checking the inventory. But all that's changed now. I'd quit today if I could—be a farmer, anything. Before, the hard work was worth it, but today there is only anarchy in commerce. There is no advancement without speculation or special privileges.

"Commerce is no longer a profession, it's no longer decent work. Everything is rotten. If there was total liberty in trade, then it might be all right. But all that one finds are regulations, taxes, inspection. I pay huge amounts in profits tax, and if I don't calculate them myself the state makes me pay a forfeitry tax whether I make a profit or not. So I hire an accountant to figure my taxes who costs me 240,000 francs [$480] a year. Even then there's always a mistake in the calculations, and the *inspecteurs* are always there to threaten you with fines if you don't placate them.

"All these regulations are applied by bureaucrats who don't understand a thing about commerce. All our taxes are gobbled up by the state to pay these bureaucrats. It would be all right if they used these taxes for investing in the economy, but no such luck. I went to the big state sugar refinery at Beni Mellal once, and there they've got mountains of sugar being destroyed by the humidity. Why is that? Because those aren't businessmen, they're bureaucrats with university degrees and they don't have any idea what sugar is. They come to work at 8:30 and leave at 5:30. They're clock watchers. Did you ever hear of an entrepreneur who was a clock watcher? Never! These bureaucrats don't have the joy of trade.

"There's a story about COSUMA which I think is true.

One day a woman bought some sugar from her grocer. Later she found a wood splinter in it, so she took it to the grocer who gave her some other sugar. The grocer took the splinter to the wholesaler, and the wholesaler took it to the factory. The manager called in the woman, and when she arrived he assembled all the workers on the plant floor. The manager held up the splinter and said, 'This woman found a splinter in our sugar. If that happens again I'll fire the man responsible.' Now that's the way business should be done. You have to take responsibility for your product, and the state can't do that.

"The state directs everything but it doesn't know what it's doing. Everything has to be paid for. There have been fifteen ministers of commerce since independence, each one worse than the last. The only thing that interests them is import licenses and graft.

"The number of people without talent who have made fortunes since independence is astounding. Most of them have been Fassi-s. What do they do? They take a room in a hotel and call it a business office. And then they take their briefcases and go from office to office until they find someone they know who can fix up an import license for them. Then in one fell swoop they make a killing. The next step for them is to speculate in urban real estate.

"Look at the X Company [a private Moroccan firm that assembles a European make of cars and trucks for the Moroccan market]. They hardly put anything together themselves. Everything is imported pre-packaged and practially assembled. The factory only uses about twenty workers. Yet their trucks are the best in Morocco and they sell for a lot of money. But where they really make money is on spare parts. They have exclusive rights to import the vehicles and the spare parts. When one of their trucks is wrecked they go to the owner and give him a new one free and take away the wreck. All that so that some junk man won't strip down the wreck and put a lot of spare parts on the market. Everything is based on privileges like that now. The way things stand now I hope that my son goes into anything but commerce."

Hadj Brahim endorses the notion that a man should work hard for what he gets, and that an individual's efforts should not be thwarted by uncomprehending and essentially unnecessary bureaucracies. Yet Hadj Brahim himself moved into wholesaling on the strength of an administrative favor, and he was not reluctant to profit, albeit in a small way, from the black market. Most Soussi-s would probably share his advocacy of hard work, frugality, respect for the customer, and responsibility for the merchandise. But the "joy of trade" on the one hand, and the need to survive, on the other, have placed the Swasa, like J'ha, in some embarrassing situations. Such a case was the cooking oil scandal of 1959, in which we find our old protagonists—the Fassi-s, the Swasa, and the Jews—pooling their cleverness to do in themselves as well as a fair number of their clients.

In October, 1959, hospitals in the Meknes region and elsewhere treated 10,823 people for a form of food-poisoning that often produced semi or total paralysis in its victims. The cause was eventually traced to cooking oil prepared and bottled at Meknes by one Moulay Idriss ben Moulay Abd, originally from the Ait Baha in the Sous. In April, 1960, Moulay Abd was brought to trial along with twenty-seven other people accused of having put on the market a food product unfit for human consumption.

What had happened was that the cooking oil, put out under a well known brand name, was debased with a highly poisonous aviation fuel. When the Nouasser SAC base outside of Casablanca was being closed down, the American authorities there had sold the fuel at auction. The oil when it left the base was clearly marked poisonous, but all the accused steadfastly denied any knowledge of its toxic nature and passed the buck to others for not having informed them.

Moulay Abd told the court that his acquaintance Hadj Lahoucine (also from the Ait Baha) a wholesaler at Sefrou and Casablanca, had tipped him off about the oil, suggesting that its low price made it a good buy. Moulay Abd tasted a sample which he found pretty awful but decided to buy several thousand litres anyway. He told his workers to mix one part of this oil to nine parts of his normal blend. Once this was done, and once he began to hear about all the cases of food poisoning in Meknes, he decided to hold the oil off the market without saying a word to the police. He swore, however, that he had no idea that the oil was not fit for consumption.

The buck passed to the wholesaler at Sefrou, who denied all responsibility, having assumed himself that the oil was edible, and finally came to rest with Hadj Abdullah Bennani, a Fassi merchant at Casablanca who dealt in lubricants and motor oils. He had bought a large allotment of the oil from the base. Bennani was outraged that he was accused of any misconduct. He had sold the oil to several people without any specific warning as to its nature. "Why should I have said anything? Anybody who comes to my warehouse knows what I handle. There is a sign on my warehouse with letters three feet high, in Arabic and French, saying 'Motor Oils and Lubricants.' Now why should I imagine that my customers are going to use that stuff for cooking oil?"

A number of Soussi retailers were brought before the

court, accused of having sold the oil even when they knew it was unfit for consumption. One had a shop assistant who keeled over, paralyzed from having eaten an egg fried in it, but continued to sell it anyway. Another who had tasted the oil and had been horrified by the flavor was asked by the judge, "But don't you cook with that oil yourself? That brand is generally the best and the cheapest at Meknes." "Your honor," replied the accused, "I only use Lesieur [the most expensive French oil]." The judge remarked, "I thought economizing was a fundamental principle of commerce, and Lesieur is much more expensive than your oil." "Staying alive is another principle of commerce," the grocer noted.

Two more of the accused were the Benchekroun brothers, Fassi hair oil manufacturers at Casablanca. They had mixed the fuel oil in their brilliantine, and an alarming number of cases of almost instantaneous baldness had been reported in Casablanca. David Ohayon, a Jew, had told the Benchekrouns that the oil was available, and he had heard about it from his associate Mordechai Benkhalifa, who had bought several thousand litres "without knowing what was in the cans." In any case he and Ohayon assured the Benchekrouns that the oil was perfect for brilliantine. The Benchekrouns sent a sample of the oil to an official state laboratory at Casablanca which notified them that the oil was indeed fit for use in the brilliantine. The Benchekrouns insisted in court that their product was excellent, and they requested the judge's permission to use some on themselves in court. The judge refused the request saying, "It would be criminal on my part to let you do so."

This could all have been comic opera—a string of J'ha's hoist on their own petard—had it not been for the ten thousand victims. The court was not amused by the antics of the accused and condemned four of them—all Swasa—to death. The sentences were never carried out. "None of us defended those men," Hadj Brahim stated. "What they did was totally dishonest and reprehensible. We did, however, try to convince the authorities not to execute them. In 1965, when the King visited Tafrawt, some well-known Swasa spoke to him about those men, pointing out that his noble ancestors all the way back to the Prophet had always demonstrated their clemency. The men had made a terrible mistake, but all that was in the past, and they had learned their lesson. The King seemed to agree, and in any case they were all pardoned later on."

It would be unfair to suggest that scandals of this kind are typical of Soussi commercial practice. To the best of my knowledge nothing of the same magnitude, gravity, and utter irresponsibility can be attributed to Moroccan tradesmen in recent decades. Yet the cooking oil affair does demonstrate the easy transition from commercial assiduity and entrepreneurial flair to criminal marketing procedures and disregard for the customer. With less serious consequences the same amalgam of business ethic and malpractice seem common to Soussi tradesmen as a whole. In this vein, little separates the Soussi merchant-entrepreneur from his nineteenth century counterpart in the United States or Europe.

The proceedings of the trial also underscore the ease with which elite members of different ethnic and religious groups can interact to share in the benefits of a commercial undertaking. In this instance, even the state was an accomplice, and, as I am sure Hadj Brahim would have predicted, bungled the job—or was paid to bungle the job—through faulty laboratory analysis.

HADJ BRAHIM VS. DAVID McCLELLAND

The overwhelming majority of societies are achievement oriented, even where roles are heavily ascribed, and
the maximization of satisfaction principle is at work in all
of them. What differs . . . is the legitimate field of achievement and the factual manifestation of satisfaction. Societies
regard different acts in different ways, but reward something they always do; and men differ in their wants.

In addition, men in all societies must organize their resources and take risks in doing so: the entrepreneurial
function is omnipresent and a condition of any form of
life. . . .

Achievement orientation, maximization, enterprise, and
capital investment are not, therefore, characteristics which
have to be created *de novo* as is often naively assumed.
Rather, the task of modernization is to harness these principles to a new institutional complex, and to put them to
work in an altered context.

CYRIL BELSHAW[5]

"Monsieur, there is no sentiment in commerce. The
only principle is to make as much money as possible and
spend the least. I always check the market to see what I
can buy most cheaply. Not so that I can put the difference
in my pocket but so that I can sell at the lowest price. The
man who sells cheapest will always have customers."

The ability to sell cheaper has always been the strength
of the Swasa. One student of Moroccan entrepreneurship
estimates that they will content themselves with a profit
margin less than half that found tolerable by a Fassi in-

[5] Cyril Belshaw, *Traditional Exchange and Modern Markets*,
(Prentice-Hall, 1965), pp. 110–111.

vestor.[6] The Fassi, Hadj Brahim would point out, if he buys cheap will still sell at high prices, thinking that he will maximize profits that way. But the Soussi is different. He never misses a sale no matter how insignificant. "The true tradesman never lets a customer escape to someone else. If he lets a customer go, it's because there is absolutely nothing to be gained in trying to keep him. The Fassi always wants to make a big deal, lots of money all at once, but the Soussi is patient and makes lots of little deals. We have a saying that 'the river is made up of raindrops.' There's another one that every grocer knows, 'Pennies are the children of *douros*; he who chases the children from his shop, will never see their mother.' "

Hadj Brahim was talking in this vein in response to a number of propositions from McClelland's book, and his reactions to them contained some interesting commentary on his approach to trade. Here are a few test propositions.

 1. *I prefer to risk a little to make a lot. That way if you are right one out of every five times, you stand to do very well.*

"That's pure speculation and speculation isn't commerce. Big risks are not part of real commerce."

 2. *Merchandise is worth whatever people will pay to buy it.*

"Yes, of course, how could it be otherwise? That's part of the normal risk every merchant has to accept. What's a banana worth? Bananas are perishable merchandise. Let's say a man imports a shipment of bananas, and when they arrive he finds the market is already full of bananas. Well, he's going to sell them for anything he can get before they spoil. If they arrive when there are no bananas on the mar-

[6] Berrada, "L'entrepreneur marocain," p. 133.

ket, he stands to make a lot of money. In both cases it's the same banana.

"You know, imports are always a risk, perhaps an intelligent one, but always a risk. For instance, when there are quotas on the importation of certain kinds of goods, you go and make application to import a quantity that is a fraction of the quota. But you may not know what the total quota is nor how many licenses are being issued. You arrange with wholesalers and demi-wholesalers to market the merchandise, and then when it arrives you find that several others have done the same thing and the wholesalers won't meet the price you had counted on. Importers usually have ulcers unless they have powerful friends."

3. *Age should take priority, rather than competence, in determining promotions.*

"Not at all. None of us would be where we are today if that were true. The elderly should be respected, but competence is more important than age."

4. *The level of education of a person should be a determining factor in what he earns.*

"In a way, I suppose that's true, but it's his level of education in his profession that counts. An illiterate can be an excellent tradesman. He may be able to carry all his inventory in his head, know all the daily wholesale prices, and remember every bit of credit he extended to his customers. That's education in the profession."

5. *There is no such thing as luck in life. Luck is something that each individual must create for himself.*

"That's true more or less. Luck never comes all by itself. One should do everything possible to prepare the way, and leave the rest to luck. A man has to invest, use his money intelligently. We have a saying that goes, 'The money of other people is blind; it must be guided by your own.' Still there's never total equality in this world, and some people have been luckier than others. Everyone at some time has good luck or bad luck."

6. *It seems to me that I waste a lot of my time uselessly.*

"Yes, that's true—but it's beyond my control. I've spent many hours without clients, and now I hardly do any business at all on Fridays, Saturdays, and Sundays. At least I learned to read and write when the shop was empty."

7. *Today, given the state of the world, the intelligent man should live for today and let tomorrow take care of itself.*

"I can't predict the future. Man always wants a better life. Man conserves for the future. There are only three animals that do this: men, rats and ants. If each man knew on what day he would die, nobody would ever do anything."

8. *As soon as I've finished a job, I don't relax, but take up another one immediately.*

"Yes, that's what I do—even if what I had just finished was unsuccessful. Because, you see, after each loss there is a gain, and after each gain a loss. It's just like women and pregnancies. Each time we forget their fatigue and begin again."

9. *In each task that I undertake, I never stop working until I'm satisfied with the results.*

"Before, it was like that, but now, it's as I have said. It's hard to have ambition any more. The privileges and the controls on the one hand, and anarchy on the other. What you find now is that everyone wants credit, and most of them get it. They don't have the sense of responsibility that we used to have. Because of all the credit, it's impossible to tell the son of a poor man from the son of a rich man. Everyone buys what they want with the money of others. These people don't sleep at night any more. Every day they have to go find the money of others to pay their debts. They buy houses, and clothes, and go to the movies. For each good thing there is something evil, but they do not see the evil until it is too late. As for me, there are no problems. I only spend my own money. I live in an apartment and not a house. I don't have a fortune, but at least I sleep soundly every night.

"But what can one expect. We have these problems because we're part of the civilization now, and we have to pay the price. These hippies are like rats; they don't hurt anyone but they ruin everything. The Moroccans are becoming like that. The young are all going astray and they're 50 percent of the population. Even the young Swasa. They have forgotten their religion, and they no longer have the traditions, the Soussi mentality. Recently there were two students here at the Law Faculty whose fathers are both from Aguerdoudad. These boys had lived most of their lives at Casablanca, and they became friends at the Faculty. Well, last year each one went back to Aguerdoudad for *Id al-Kebir*. They met each other on the bus. One said, 'Where are you going?' The other said, 'Aguerdoudad.' So the other said, 'What do you know, so am I!' All those years together and neither had thought to ask where the other was born! These youngsters don't know anything about their origins. They don't even know the names of their grandfathers.

"Now they get married without asking their parents' opinion. At least they don't marry Christians or Jews. But I can tell you that I hope my son asks my permission before he gets married. And you know it's harder and harder to tell the Swasa apart from the others. We look, and talk, and dress just like the others. It's not like the Fassi-s. As soon as a Fassi opens his mouth you know who he is.

"So Morocco is becoming modern, but I'm pessimistic. There's been a terrible regression in morality. Religion and tradition don't count for anything any more. We send students all over the world, and they come back and have to form some sort of mixture. They have a chance to be true scientists, but all they want to be are bureaucrats so that they can have power and feel important."

INTERMEDIARIES, GROUP SOLIDARITY, AND "NON-RATIONAL" BEHAVIOR

A large, red, mud-splattered Berliet truck ground up the main road toward the central square of Tafrawt. Hadj Qassim, standing in front of his shop, did not seem to notice the truck. His attention was fixed on the mud and rivulets of water that were making their way towards the entrance of his depot at the bottom of the gently sloping square. A fine drizzle was falling, and it was cold even though it was late March. The Jebel Lkist even had a few tattered patches of snow on its barren face.

Hadj Qassim stared out disconsolately, his paunch thrust forward, hands behind his back, as the tide of mud edged toward his shop. He had not bothered to trim his thin white fringe beard nor to put on a clean jellaba, even though it was the day after *Id al-Kebir*. He often thought that accepting the wholesaling license the French offered him in 1941—in return for his information and expertise on his tribesmates—was a mixed blessing. Twenty-six years of security (for it was now 1967) and local prestige did not always seem worth the sacrifice of the excitement of

Casablanca, where he had started off his career as a grocer in the 1920s. A diabetic, he suffered stoically his fate as sugar wholesaler, but it would have been so much easier to put up with the interminable tea-drinking of his friends had he been in Casablanca rather than Tafrawt, which came to life only a few times each year.

One had to step down to enter Hadj Qassim's shop. Behind him, inside the somber storehouse, an assortment of young assistants scurried about, lifting sacks of sugar cones to higher ground, clearing the dirt floor of all perishable items, stacking bags of chick peas, spices, boxes of tea, matches, and the like on top of the battered counter or on barrels of olive oil.

The red Berliet came to a halt directly in front of Hadj Qassim, who scarcely looked up. In the back of the truck, under a tarpaulin, were a hundred or so cases containing gallon tins of cooking oil. A young man, twenty years old perhaps, with a light moustache, leapt out of the cab and hurried over to greet the Hadj, shaking his hand and then touching his own to his lips and his breast in deference to the older man. A stream of greetings and inquiries as to the health of the Hadj and his family poured forth in *tashilhit*, for the young man was from the Ammiln himself. Hadj Qassim replied perfunctorily, one eyebrow arched as he watched the young man. The latter chattered on about the weather, the difficulty of bringing the oil up from the depot at Tiznit, the rain, but receiving little response from the Hadj, he pulled a sheaf of papers out of the breast pocket of his smock, suggesting that the Hadj might sign them to indicate receipt of the cooking oil he had ordered. The Hadj merely stared at him inscrutably. The young man appeared somewhat ill at ease and asked if the shop assistants might not unload the truck, and once the Hadj had verified the shipment, he could then sign the papers. Hadj Qassim said: "The truck will not be unloaded."

Down the dirt street that the truck had just climbed, one could see the various retailers whose shops lined the street, sneaking glimpses of the little drama that was taking place. "But Hadj, I don't understand. What do you mean? You ordered the oil, didn't you? And here it is, right on time, despite the floods. A little muddy, I'll admit, but here it is." Hadj Qassim remained impervious. The young man seized his hand and with the other fingered a fold of cloth on the Hadj's jellaba, talking all the while, pulling the Hadj away from the shop entrance for a short stroll under the porticos that ran along the square. This maneuver terminated, the young man was clearly distraught. He flung his arms wide apart, and pleaded with the Hadj to accept his delivery, otherwise he would surely be fired by his boss back in Tiznit. "You deserve it," the Hadj stated with finality. All heads along the street were turned towards the scene as the young man, crestfallen, climbed back in the cab of the truck and began the long drive back to Tiznit. The Hadj shot an imperious glance down the street. The shop-keepers looked away or busied themselves with other tasks.

The sin of the young man was simple enough, one that recurs constantly throughout the entire Moroccan commercial network. Before rounding the corner to climb the hill to Hadj Qassim's wholesale depot, the truck stopped in front of a small grocery run by the driver's cousin. There, about ten tins of oil were quickly unloaded before the truck moved on to its final destination. The cousin obtained oil at the manufacturer's price and deprived the Hadj of a sale. Not a very big one to be sure, but if all the retailers bought directly from the manufacturer, who would need a wholesaler at Tafrawt? The Hadj's grapevine had informed

Some Soussi men.

Foreground: village houses.
Middle ground: Ammiln Valley with argan trees.
Background: Jebel Lkist.

A village of the Ammiln.
Foreground: *argan* trees. House to left
with characteristic ornamental door.

The village agglomeration of Iskouzrou.

An *agadir* or communal grain house in the region of the Ait Baha.

The city of Casablanca and its port.
Left foreground: old *medina*.
Right and middle ground: the modern city.

Route de Strasbourg on a quiet morning.

Soussi wholesaler's shop: oil, tea, soap, sugar.
Just off the Route de Strasbourg, Casablanca.

Fassi cloth wholesalers, Route de Strasbourg.

The old *medina* as seen from new buildings
along the Avenue des Forces Armées Royales, Casablanca.

The *bidonville* of Carrières Centrales.
Left foreground: the bidonville itself.
Right: housing development.
Left and right middle ground: housing of the new *medina* variety.

A street in the bidonville of Ben M'sik.

The shop of a retailer—a woodseller—in the bidonville of Ben M'sik.

him of the truck driver's sin even before the truck stopped in front of his shop. The Hadj had no choice but to react firmly in the face of this breach of conduct. His glance down the street was fair warning to the other retailers that such practices should not be repeated.

The simplification and "rationalization" of trade networks through the elimination of superfluous intermediaries (I do not mean to suggest that Hadj Qassim is superfluous) might be a desirable phenomenon making for a more responsive distribution system and probably lower retail prices. Yet Moroccans feel instinctively that the price of rationalization is too high to pay. Moroccans in general, not just Swasa or retailers, act in such a way as to proliferate intermediaries in most social and economic activities. Networks must absorb as many people as possible, and a ridiculously small sum of initial capital may stretch itself out to a multitude. In Morocco, all systems are saturated; there are too many of everybody: too many unemployed, too many peasants, too many bureaucrats, too many retailers. Most people with incomes are aware of and disturbed by this situation.

The proliferation of intermediaries is a compensatory device to soak up some of the excess. In effect, the intermediaries perform services, perhaps not vital ones but services nonetheless, and they ensure their own subsistence when other forms of work are unavailable. Parasite or marginal trades and services require little or no investment or overhead. In the shantytowns, for instance, there are men (*mul an-nukhala*) who gather stale bread in the well-off districts of town and sell it by the pound to bakers in the slums, who reconstitute the bread for the local clientele. In country markets, there are self-appointed middlemen who buy grain from individual peasants as they arrive at market, postponing payment until the end of the day. Once the middlemen have assembled several bushels, they sell the grain to wholesalers for a slight markup per bushel. When they have been paid, they in turn pay off the individual peasants and keep the difference. In the cities, a man may go to the wholesale market and "borrow" a crate of melons or vegetables for the day. He then will try to unload the produce in the residential quarters of town, going from door to door. If he is successful, he will pay back the wholesaler in the evening and keep whatever profit he may have made. One could go on with a myriad of other parasite trades, from ragpickers to car-watchers. In all these instances the "tradesman" can start with nothing—no capital, fixed or liquid, and no license—and yet with some luck, wind up with money in his pocket.[7]

From near nothing, then, a vast tertiary sector of marginal services and trades is created. It is like a bucket brigade in which everyone sips from the bucket before passing it on. The fire is never put out, but the thirst raised by the work is partially quenched. To disperse the bucket brigade and bring in a fire truck would prove nothing if there is no pressure in the mains. The fire would rage on, the people would be thirsty and the truck idle.[8]

Consequently, it is considered reprehensible, if not immoral, to eliminate intermediaries and to consolidate ex-

[7] In 1960, there were over 38,000 *licensed* tradesmen in Casablanca, that is, over 19 per cent of all employed males. There were thus 42 tradesmen for every 1,000 residents of the city. One may suppose that for every licensed tradesman there was *at least* one without a license. For an exhaustive treatment, see Kingdom of Morocco, Haut Commissariat au Plan, *Etude sur le Commerce Intérieur*, 3 vols., (Rabat: Division des Statistiques et du Plan, 1968).

[8] Cf. Geertz, *Peddlers and Princes*, p. 31 on Indonesian intermediaries.

change systems, that is, to tamper with the survival system. To do so is like taking bread from the mouths of the poor. Hadj Brahim once lamented the growing sophistication of grocery store operations and the gradual emergence of the supermarket. "There is too much amalgamation in trade and commerce. Even a vegetable seller sells lots of other things too, from cleaning rags to pins and needles. With this kind of commerce everyone has to work extremely hard to make a profit and as a result a lot of people lose. It was better before. I'd just as soon sell one thing, say mint. I would be able to live on that, and there would be room for others."

In a system of distribution that is overstaffed, the resulting parasitism is not confined to those at the bottom of the hierarchy, but is shared at all levels. Wholesaler, retailer, and pushcart salesman can all become superfluous and are all aware, to varying degrees, of this fact. The shared sense of vulnerability, while not reducing all members of the system to equality, does promote a sense of tolerance among the participants, and a general awareness of the costs of consolidation.

The Hadj Qassim episode is illustrative of some other themes as well. In anecdotal form it reveals the constant rivalry that the tribal framework can contain at a level where the concept of tribal solidarity is of very little use. Conversely, and at another level, it demonstrates the utility of the tribal referent—which in similar circumstances could just as easily be the lineage, the family, or the ethnic referent —in introducing an element of predictability into social and economic relations.

One of the standard propositions David McClelland has employed to measure levels of n-achievement in groups and individuals all over the world is the following: "In the final analysis, in commerce one can have confidence only in one's friends and relatives." When I asked Hadj Brahim for his reaction to this, he said, "Of course that's true, and friends are more important than relatives." In this respect then, the Hadj is retrograde, a potential underachiever, an obstacle to rational economic activity. Here is how McClelland analyzes this attitude:

> The item labeled "market morality" is particularly interesting in view of the importance we assigned to this factor for economic growth. . . . The Americans disagree almost completely with this sentiment (ie., that you can only trust friends and relatives, J.W.) or . . . they believe that you can trust strangers significantly more than do managers in any of the other countries. . . . Fair dealings in the market with impersonal, unrelated "others" (i.e., strangers) is one of the necessities of advanced economic organization. If, on the other hand, prices, contracts, supplies, etc. are a function of a multiplicity of particularistic relationships with friends, enemies, or compadres—in a word, of personal alliances—then economic efficiency is bound to suffer.[9]

Hadj Brahim and Hadj Qassim would argue that the Soussi way is economically more efficient than the trust-in-strangers approach. The Swasa can enforce a number of practices among themselves without recourse to the courts, the police, or lawyers. They obtain fairly rapid results in matters that would otherwise drag on for months in the courts, and cost large sums in fees and bribes, without any assurance that a just verdict would be forthcoming. In the general situation in which the Swasa must operate, the particularist ties deplored by McClelland speed up transactions and encourage conformity to certain commercial

[9] McClelland, *Achieving Society*, p. 291.

practices.[10] Swasa tradesmen have covered the debts of individual members of the community so that no Soussi at Casablanca has ever been declared bankrupt.[11] And bankruptcy, according to Hadj Brahim "is total dishonor and a living death." Thus, the particularist ties of the Swasa provide a financial cushion that may be considerably more dependable than that offered by banks or "impersonal" creditors.

Perhaps of greater significance is the fact that the Swasa would be reluctant to approach these problems in terms of trust and confidence. The Soussi tradesman probably has confidence and trust in *no one*. Relatives and friends can be untrustworthy. What the Soussi seeks is that situation in which *sanctions* can be most easily and quickly brought to bear upon the careless. In their eyes, that situation is almost always "particularistically" defined. Hadj Qassim's imperious glance down the street at his tribesmates would have been lost on "impersonal others."

[10] Abner Cohen makes a similar argument for the efficiency of Hausa ethnicity or tribalism in urban trade. See his *Custom and Politics in Urban Africa: A Study of Hausa Migrants in Yoruba Towns* (Berkeley and Los Angeles: University of California Press, 1969), pp. 180–200.

[11] See Adam, *Casablanca*, I, 373.

Chapter V

La "Boulitique"

When the tempest blows in the land of the palm trees
The highest branches are shaken the most violently
So much the worse for you, eagle, perched on top of
The tree.

SONG OF AL-HIBA[1]

CASABLANCA is one of the four largest cities on the African continent—1,500,000 inhabitants in 1970—yet at the time of the establishment of the French protectorate in 1912, it was a fishing port of 20,000 souls. As a result, the city is in most respects brand new, but, despite its newness, it has a character of its own. It is one of those "primate" cities, common to the developing countries, that monopolize so much of the urban population that urban centers of intermediate size are stunted in their growth. In 1968, about one in every ten Moroccans lived at Casablanca, as did one in every three urbanites.

Downtown Casablanca, the business and hotel district, could be anywhere in the European Mediterranean. There is a little bit of Marseille, a little bit of Nice, a little bit of Algiers, but other than the tomb of Sidi Belyout, in a little park at the entrance to the port area, there is little that is Moroccan. The oldest European buildings, dating from about 1920, are low structures with ornamental balconies

---

[1] Justinard, *Caid Goundafi*, p. 250.

and cornices. But the landscape is dominated by the ten- and fifteen-story buildings that went up in the boom years after the Second World War. They march along the broad Avenue of the Royal Armed Forces up to the Place Mohammed V, formerly the Place de France. Just on the other side of the square is the Old Medina where the original 20,000 were living when French soldiers first landed in 1907. In 1960, 136,000 people had managed to find room in a somewhat expanded version of the Old Medina.

The city grew out from the Place de France in all directions. Europeans lived in the central residential areas and then edged south toward Anfa and Ain Diab, the Gold Coast and Nob Hill in one. Poorer Europeans, such as the Spanish, lived in more modest surroundings in the center of the new town. The district known as Ma'arif became the stronghold of the Spanish, and the "poor white" outlook of its inhabitants made it something akin to Algiers' Bab al-Oued. By the 1930s, the French had helped develop a sprawling Muslim residential area called the Nouvelle Medina, a jumble of two- and three-story buildings that contained a population of 185,000 in 1960.

Similar clusters of buildings in the same style have developed over the years, some with official guidance, others through private auspices. The new cities house the bulk of Casablanca's population, consisting of the lower middle class workers, clerks, government employees, school teachers, and tradesmen. In Morocco, just about anyone who earns a salary can claim middle class status. It is not surprising then that one finds fairly high concentrations of Swasa in the new cities and quarters such as Sidi Othman, Derb Ghallef, Bouchentouf, Moulay Cherif, and the Nouvelle Medina itself. Here, the urban nationalist movement first took root and found its ablest recruits. Perhaps in building the Nouvelle Medina, the French wished to seal off the native population from the European downtown area as much as possible. But their success in this respect turned on them, for they found it difficult to penetrate their own creation when it was transformed into a base of operations for urban terror.

In their efforts to house the natives, the French were also concerned by the sudden growth of shanty towns on the outskirts of the city. The first camps were implanted in the 1920s and grew alarmingly in the 1930s. These shanty towns became known as *bidonvilles* because one essential building material used in the construction of the shacks is tin cans (*bidons*) beaten flat to form a sort of shingle. The largest shanty-towns are Carrières Centrales (59,000 people in 1959), near the city's industrial zone and housing thousands of workers, and at Ben M'sik (97,000 in 1959) somewhat further out along the Route de Mediouna where the shackdwellers have a tantalizing view of downtown Casablanca.[2] Other shanty towns developed wherever a proprietor was willing to rent out his land for that purpose. The municipal authorities have never recognized the legality of these structures, so no shackdweller would risk transforming his shack into a permanent dwelling for fear that it would be razed. Harassed by the authorities, emigrants have built shacks inside of shacks, in the interior wells of houses in the medinas, or just about anywhere a little space could be found and the blind eye of the authorities assured. Today 400,000 *Casablancais* live in shacks, that is, 28 percent of the city's population.

[2] See André Adam, "Le bidonville de Ben M'sik à Casablanca," *Annales de l'Institut d'Etudes Orientales*, VIII (1949–1950), 61–198; also Cdt. R. Maneville, "Prolétariat et bidonvilles," Centre de Hautes Etudes sur l'Afrique et l'Asie Moderne (Paris), LXIII, 1712 (April, 1950); unpublished.

The city's limits enclose an area as large as Paris, but judging from the physical expansion of the city in the outlying quarters, Casablanca will need every inch it can get. Proceeding away from the center of town, one moves into another world, a world of sprawling *bidonvilles* and housing developments, of vast new nouvelles medina-s, of factories and empty fields farmed until recently in the face of the oncoming city. The outskirts are at once desolate and surging with life. The buildings arise out of naked ground and rubble, like reconstruction after heavy bombing. The rubble is everywhere: trash and litter, remains of older buildings, refuse from downtown. The main boulevards are paved, lined as far as the eye can see with two- and three-story squarish buildings whose upper stories hang out over the first. The vivid colors frequently used for trim do little to relieve the drabness of the scene.

Among the buildings, in the rubble, the dust, or the mud of winter, swarm the several hundred thousand inhabitants of these quarters. The streets, the empty lots, the outdoor markets are, as the French put it, *fourmillant*, or crawling as with ants. The ground floor of all the buildings is occupied by grocery stores, hardware shops, or workshops aclatter with bicycle and automobile repairs. The streets are full of nonchalant pedestrians oblivious to the droves of motorbikes and hurtling buses. Any patch of ground more than twenty yards long hosts an army of urchins, lost in the clouds of dust raised by their determined efforts to play soccer. A giant crater near the Route de Mediouna, is filled partially with murky water, and its sides are dotted with the women of the shanty towns, there to do their wash. In the rubble-filled fields, men spread dyed wool to dry, as donkeys and mules rummage about for something to eat. Across the Route de Mediouna is the Suq al-Koria, a giant market of shacks, where the shackdwellers come to buy.

These are ghettos, animated and ominous, that may some day swallow Casablanca. In them exists a subculture in which people have lived for years, in semi-isolation from the heart of the city itself. The people are hostile to outsiders but not defiant, for they are vulnerable and have much to lose. The city, whether or not they have work, is better than the countryside. They do not want to be sent back. Practically every aspect of their lives is subject to administrative control: permission to live in a shack, work permits, identity papers, entrance of children in schools, trade licenses, and so forth. They must be careful, or they may lose whatever the city may have to offer them.

In a recent report, a government agency urged that the Ministry of Interior be more solicitous towards the denizens of the *bidonvilles*, because, probably for the reasons stated above, it was felt that they are a "conservative force." Indeed, Maoists are not likely to make much headway in Casablanca's *bidonvilles*, where the problems of survival are too acute to leave much room for militancy. These people live by bread alone, but breadless "conservatives" have ransacked other Middle Eastern cities and did so in Casablanca in 1965. Driss Chraibi, whose novels tell more about Moroccan urban society than most scholarly works, describes the mood of the *bidonvilles*, or, as he puts it, "the zone."[3]

> Not by bread alone, somebody said. He could. It was an image, a symbol, but he could certainly say it. The socialist camp could afford the luxury of claiming that he needed something other than bread. Here, in the zone, there was no bread. Not a crumb. Nothing but a swampy and sub-socialist humanity whose members succeeded in develop-

[3] Driss Chraibi, *Succession Ouverte*, (Paris: Denoel, 1962), pp. 153–155. See also his extraordinary *Le Passé Simple*, (Paris, 1954).

ing their bone structure, but that was all. And children, flocks of children, up before the sun and running naked, stomaches distended and immense eyes, searching for garbage. If they found some crumbs, it was God's blessing. But they found tracts. They brought back trachoma, staphylococcus, and that resignation to whatever trial, imposed by whatever adult ideology. Here, these children, and those who were waiting for them to come back, have but one ideal: to be able to say one day that they had enough bread to live. . . .

If bread was lacking, there was the refuse that society had no use for: rusty tin cans and old rotten boards. The boards became walls, the cans cut with scissors became rooves of the huts. But all these living bones awaited a revolutionary ideology to transform them into lead soldiers. . . . They were hunched over, limb by limb, in front of their huts, facing the sun that rose East of Eden and that set every day West of this Eden. But doubtless at sunrise and sunset, those who ate other than bread, looked out further than the sun.

Transistor radios poured mysticism and statisticism on the zone, production norms and hymns. Ears could still hear and mouths salivate, the bellies digesting the sounds of all these good things of life; all these consumer goods that the East and the West claimed to possess, and that they throw in your face before dropping bombs and rockets. Both were of the same race. They could either make war or love. Here, there was another humanity. Sometimes, a ray of sun came to illuminate the portrait of a leader deep inside a shack. And thus it was: the portrait was smashed to pieces and thrown in the stream of slimy water that flowed between the shacks.

Almost as soon as the rural centers of resistance to the French presence had been pacified, the cities took up the slack. The southern mountains were conquered in 1934, but already in 1930 the young bourgeois nationalists of Fez had launched their movement. Tribal resistance, cast in the traditional mold of opposition to any central authority, rapidly gave way to distinctly modern forms of resistance and organization. The nationalists brought politics—*la boulitique* in Moroccan argot—to the cities, with parties and cells, newspapers and labor unions, ideology and tracts. The Swasa laid down their arms in 1934, but many participated in the first major industrial strike of Moroccan workers: that against COSUMA in 1936.

Hadj Brahim made this transition himself. His first political act had been to take up arms against the French in the Ait Abdullah. Most of his tribesmates were already long familiar with this form of "political participation." A goodly number, however, who were in trade in the cities, followed Brahim into the unfamiliar and dangerous realm of *la boulitique*, taking on the French with the paraphernalia of the industrial state built around political parties and urban resistance, and meeting their counterparts in the army and the police. The major arena for the political transformation of the Swasa was Casablanca, a city almost exclusively of recent migrants among whom the Chleuh of the High and Anti-Atlas and the Sahara were heavily represented. Because Casablanca is the commercial and industrial hub of Morocco, its politics became to an important degree synonymous with that of the nation as a whole.

In the years following World War II, the nationalist movement expanded from a fairly narrow bourgeois base to absorb large numbers of the urban lower middle class, workers, and even shackdwellers. Casablanca, the heart of the French economic presence, was naturally a primary target of the nationalists. To no small extent the Fassi merchant bourgeoisie of Casablanca financed the growth of the mass movement. Their vehicle was the Istiqlal party, which they partially controlled, but their cadres and their recruits were almost necessarily non-Fassi. The Fassi-s had money but not numbers. The effort required to put together a mass, city-based party was turned over to young intellectuals of modest origins and to "little people" like Hadj Brahim. They established the link between the new cities and the shanty towns (particularly Carrières Centrales) that rendered the native quarters hostile to the French presence.

The shift from elite to mass politics took place within the trade community of Casablanca as well as in the population as a whole. The French encouraged this shift. Having lost an initial battle with the native bourgeoisie, they decided to introduce many more players into the game, the better to control it. In so doing the French brought the petty tradesmen of the Sous directly into urban politics.

The French tried to give the protectorate a more liberal image in the postwar years. They set up indirect elections of Moroccans to an advisory body known as the Council of Government. This council had been in existence for several years. It had a French and a Moroccan section which met separately and deliberated the economic policies of the protectorate. The French section had always been elected, but until 1947 the Moroccan section was appointed and contained only Moroccans known to be subservient to French interests. But all that was to change, for the French decided that through indirect elections and restricted suffrage the Moroccans would be permitted to select their own representatives to the council. They were to be chosen from the members of the Moroccan sections of the Chambers of Agriculture, Commerce and Industry. These in turn were to be elected by adult Moroccans legally exercising the profession of cultivator, merchant, or industrialist. In 1947

Moroccans eligible to vote for members of the Chambers of Commerce and Industry did not exceed 8,000 voters in the entire country.

The new system played into the hands of the Fassi bourgeoisie. Indirect election gave the vote to the commercial elite, and more particularly to those entrepreneurs who had hitched their wagons to the Istiqlal Party. In this situation money counted more than numbers, and in 1948, when the first elections were held, the nationalists pushed their list through both stages and on to victory in the Council of Government. Once there, they formed a compact group that harassed the French Resident-General on all policy matters pertaining to the economy. Implicitly their vocal criticisms went much further, attacking the legitimacy of the protectorate itself. In December, 1950, during a particularly stormy session of the council, one of Morocco's most successful entrepreneurs, Mohammed Laghzaoui, and one of France's most renowned officers, General Juin, at the time resident-general in Morocco, engaged in a shouting match that resulted in Laghzaoui's expulsion from the council. Laghzaoui and the other nationalists in the council immediately went to see Sultan Mohammed bin Youssef, to complain of the peremptory treatment that the resident-general had meted out to them. The council had proved to be anything but docile, and the French decided to change the rules for selecting its members.

New elections were scheduled to take place in the fall of 1951. Just two weeks before the day they were to be held, a new electoral law was published, drastically expanding the number eligible to vote for the professional chambers. Whereas in 1948 only those whose volume of business exceeded a certain level, and whose names appeared in the Commercial Register, were allowed to vote, in 1951 anyone who had a trade license, even if only to operate a pushcart, was eligible. The electorate soared from 8,000 to 220,000. The French banked on three reactions to their manoeuvre. First, they were confident that the Istiqlal could in no way organize the new mass of voters in the short time allotted. Second, they counted on a low turnout in view of the essentially illiterate and uninformed electorate. Finally, they assumed that through their protegès in the commercial world, among whom were several Swasa, they could put together a coalition that would be sufficient to beat the bourgeois elite. In the game as defined by the French numbers became more important than money.

The Istiqlal saw the trap, and avoided it by calling for a boycott of the elections. Even for this negative appeal, they needed the cooperation of the petty tradesmen, who were at the same time subjected to the pressures of the French to get out the vote. The nationalists, in the few years that they had sought mass support in the cities, had done their job well. Abstention in the elections throughout Morocco varied from 60 to 98 percent of the registered voters. In Casablanca, where there were 10,000 registered voters, only 424 turned up at the polls. Hadj Abbid was one of the candidates to the Casablanca Chamber of Commerce and was elected by this tiny band. The French had counted on Hadj Abbid and other Soussi big men to bring off their strategy. In this instance, however, the Soussi grocers decided to take their orders from the Fassi bourgeoisie. They had made an ideological choice, a choice that symbolized their entry into nationalist politics. The "old Soussi-Fassi rivalry" that the French sought to stimulate proved, this time, to be nonoperative.

The events recounted above were cast in fairly conventional terms. *La boulitique* had not yet become the violent and brutal game of the years 1952 to 1955. The Casablanca riots of December 7 to 9, 1952, put an end to that situation. Farhat Hachad, a Tunisian labor leader, had been assassinated, apparently at the hands of French terrorists; Moroccan labor leaders called for a strike in memory of their fallen brother, virtually unknown to the Moroccan masses; and, perhaps to the surprise of all concerned, Casablanca erupted. An initially peaceful workers' strike evoked strong police action followed by mob retaliation, particularly from Carrières Centrales. When order had been restored, over 3,000 Moroccans had been arrested and perhaps 300 killed.[4]

When it was all over much of the bourgeois leadership of the Istiqlal was in jail or in exile. The following summer, the Sultan, whom the French judged to be too intimate with the nationalists, was sent off to Madagascar. A doddering and bewildered cousin, Bin Arafa, was placed on the throne, where, in his efforts to please the French, he signed everything submitted to him, including, it is said, the menu for his lunch. The Moroccan elite was in confinement. The "little people" took over the movement, after their fashion.

The Casablanca Municipal Market lies in the heart of the European business and residential quarter. On Christmas morning 1953 it was bustling with last minute shoppers picking up meat, vegetables, and flowers for the Christmas feast. In the heart of the market an inconspicuous shopping basket had been left in front of the stall known as Boucherie Felix. At 11:40 A.M. the basket exploded, killing seventeen people and wounding twenty-eight. It was by no means the first terrorist attack—there had been several in the months following the Sultan's exile—but it was the most horrifying.

[4] See Stéphane Bernard, *Le Conflit Franco-Marocain: 1943–1956*, 3 vols., (Brussels, 1963) I, 135–147.

Just three days before, Sultan Bin Arafa had gathered together the *ulema* and induced them to issue an order threatening the death penalty to anyone engaged in terrorist activities. The bomb was an answer to both the Sultan and his Christian protectors.

The man who left the bomb was Mohammed Mansour, an "Arab" from a poor rural family of the Chaouia. His deed was immediately denounced by several Fassi merchants, who declared that they wished above all to "safeguard Franco-Moroccan friendship and the future of the country." Among those expressing their indignation was Mohammed Jilali Bennani. Seven years later, he and Mansour found themselves as rival candidates in the elections to the Casablanca Chamber of Commerce.

Mansour was captured in 1954 and condemned to death. When the verdict was read, he said simply: "The hopes of all Moroccans were snuffed out when the Sultan was exiled." The verdict was never carried out, as Morocco was granted independence in November, 1955. The fervor with which the "little people" fought in the name of the exiled Sultan characterized the chaotic years of resistance that preceded independence. Mohammed bin Youssef became known as the Sultan of Carrières Centrales. Despite *la boulitique*, the Moroccan proletariat still claimed a theocratic father figure as the symbol of its destiny.

Hadj Brahim had committed himself to the nationalist movement and had not shied away from the violence of the urban resistance. His role was not bomb thrower but cell organizer, fund collector, and information gatherer. His shop—or more accurately, his shops—as well as those of his allies might serve as arms cache, message drop, or refuge for a hunted terrorist. The Soussi grapevine linking Morocco's urban centers could pass on political information as easily as prices on the local sugar market. The grocers and other retailers were in constant contact with all elements of the population, from workers and slumdwellers to the police and the European well-to-do. They were the ears of the urban movement. The nationalists were able to channel supplies and arms, personnel and intelligence, through the ready-made communications systems of the various urban retail communities. The tradesmen also contributed financially to the movement. Whether they did so out of fear of reprisals or out of devotion to the cause is a question asked about virtually all resistance movements. There is probably no conclusive answer, but Hadj Brahim, who helped collect funds, is not the kind to use a shakedown. Substantial numbers of tradesmen probably tried to please both the French and the nationalists, awaiting the conclusion of the struggle and the emergence of a victor.

This *attentisme* frustrated Hadj Brahim. "There were very few Swasa who were in politics. Most of our people were frightened. The police would come and search your shop and break up your merchandise. You could be arrested without warning, and there were many summary executions. A bomb would go off or someone would be shot somewhere, and then those trucks full of Senegalese that were always patroling the town would rush off to the scene of the incident and terrorize everyone in the vicinity.

"After 1952, there really wasn't any Istiqlal in Casablanca. There were only the resistance cells with very few contacts among them. And in the popular quarters of Casablanca there was perfect order; no robberies, no rapes, no drunks. Anyone caught for such crimes might be lynched by the resistance.

"Orders would come from unknown sources, and they would be obeyed. In 1954 there was the boycott of tobacco products, which were under a French monopoly. Then the boycott was extended to all luxury goods. It hurt many petty tradesmen. The French used to give licenses for tobacco shops to Moroccan veterans of the French army. Those that accepted the licenses were sometimes executed by the resistance. And for the rest of us, it was not much better. The resistants wanted us to close our shops as a sign of protest, and of course the French wanted us to stay open as a sign of support. The *muqqadim* [an official responsible for a city quarter] and the Senegalese would come around in the morning and say, 'Why is your shutter down? Why aren't you open?' So up would go the shutter. Then a resistant would come by: 'Why are you open?' And down would go the shutter. Up, down, up, down, all day long. Finally some Swasa pulled their shutters halfway down. When the *muqqadim* came around, they told him the open half was for the French, and when the resistant came, they told him the top half was his.

"The French were using collective repression. No one was spared, and everyone was frightened. The resistance gave us hope, something to live for. Even Mansour's bomb. What could you expect? The French resorted to violence, and they bred violence. Even Hadj Abbid had to turn on the French. He was made head of a nationalist delegation that went to Paris in 1954. At a press conference at the Hotel Crillon, he demanded the return of the Sultan to Morocco. There was the resident-general's hand-picked President of the Casablanca Chamber of Commerce demanding the Sultan's return. That must have hurt.

"By 1955 the resistance had a lot of support. All the shops closed down for fifty-six days consecutively. Only the municipal markets were allowed to remain open. The resistance did let the tradesmen serve their best customers through the back of the shop. But the shutters were down for fifty-six days when the *muqqadim* came around."

In general, Brahim portrays the tradesman's role in the urban movement as a passive one with only a few active participants. Violent political acts were always undertaken by a minority, so that in such cases one deals only with reduced numbers. However, André Adam found that of two hundred and eleven Moroccans arrested in Casablanca for terrorist activities in this period, 42.5 percent (ninety) were artisans and tradesmen.[5] They constituted far and away the largest single category, followed by workers with 26 percent (fifty-five). In last place were students with 1.5 percent (three).[6] I do not know what proportion of the ninety was Swasa, nor, when dealing with such small numbers, would it be particularly significant to have exact figures. Nonetheless, one may suppose that among the militant, lower middle class minority that carried the cudgels for the nationalists at Casablanca, the Swasa played an important role. The Manouzzi brothers from near Tafrawt (Amanouz), Ahmidou Faris "al-Watani" (the Patriot) from the High Atlas, Ahmad Oulhadj, and Tahar Sidki from the Ammiln are illustrious Soussi nationalists. They helped organize the Istiqlal and the resistance both in Casablanca and the Sous itself.

When it is a question of the leadership of the Istiqlal, Hadj Brahim is not so ready to minimize the Soussi effort. "It was the Fassi-s in the party who gave all the orders and decided on strategy. But we did the work and carried the

[5] Zerktouni, the great martyr of the Casablanca resistance, was a carpenter. He committed suicide when arrested by the French.

[6] Adam, *Casablanca*, II, 557. On political behaviour in the shanty towns of the Third World see Joan Nelson, *Migrants, Urban Poverty, and Instability in Developing Nations*, (Cambridge, Mass.: C.I.A. Harvard, 1969).

heaviest load. Naturally we resented this, but for the cause we didn't want to create any disunity in the movement. After all, the Fassi-s were better educated, and with their money they could move around and see many people. They probably could see the overall situation better than us. Still we thought that with independence we would have a greater voice in the party."

The Swasa remained the forgotten men after 1956. The Fassi-s—that is, any educated, well-to-do urbanites—moved into prominant positions in the Moroccan government and administration, and, in many instances, began to feather their own nests. Traffic in licenses and favors began in earnest, and although the Swasa were not entirely excluded from a share in the spoils, the Istiqlali bourgeoisie did not seem overly grateful to the "little people."

The exiled Sultan had returned in triumph to Morocco and had become King Mohammed V. For four years he presided over party governments dominated by the Istiqlal. These years were marked by a trial of strength between the King, who wished to rule, and the party, that wished to reduce him to a symbolic role. The young intellectuals who had engineered the transformation of the Istiqlal into a mass party now devoted their energies to expanding the party's organization into all walks of life. The party sponsored professional organizations to bring unionized labor, peasants, bureaucrats, artisans, merchants, and industrialists under its aegis. If these efforts had been successful, the party would have pre-empted the King's audience, presenting the throne with a *fait accompli*.

The mastermind behind these plans was a brilliant young intellectual: Mahdi Ben Barka. One of his creations after 1956 was the National Union of Artisans, Merchants, and Industrialists (UMCIA). Although Ben Barka came from a poor family, he cooperated easily with the party bourgeoisie. In fact he entrusted the UMCIA to Mohammed Laraqi and Mohammed Jilali Bennani, two well-known Fassi entrepreneurs at Casablanca. However, Ben Barka did contact a handful of Swasa nationalists, including Hadj Brahim, to help bring petty tradesman into the new organization.

Brahim recalls going to one of the first meetings of the organizers, in a loft over the Garage Allal on the Route de Mediouna in Casablanca. There were a hundred or so people there, but few of them were Swasa. Some of them pointed out to Ben Barka that the Swasa deserved an important place in the UMCIA. Ben Barka agreed and gave them a free hand to bring in whomever they wanted. Brahim and the others willingly complied. By 1956 Brahim had become one of the unofficial political spokesmen of the Soussi community at Casablanca, a function he carries out to this day.

Once the organization came into formal existence, the Fassi leadership ran it in their own interests, readily accepting the Swasa as dues payers but not much more. The young intellectuals who encouraged the creation of the UMCIA were themselves none too pleased with the bourgeois leadership. To Ben Barka and his more militant associates, the party bourgeoisie seemed to have lost their nerve in the growing confrontation with the King. The economic spoils that independence brought were too sweet to risk in a struggle for increased political power. The old guard wanted to temporize; the militants pressed for a showdown. The Istiqlal began to break apart under the strain, particularly in 1958, and a year later came entirely unstuck. The militants walked out and established a new party—the National Union of Popular Forces—and the old bourgeoisie retained control of the remnants of the Istiqlal.

The Swasa opted for the new party almost *en masse*, albeit in their typically passive way. Here, for once, the Soussi-Fassi rivalry was operative. Strangely enough, ethnic friction became a major factor in the political rather than the economic realm. However, this distinction may be somewhat misleading, as for the Swasa politics is often commerce by another name.[7] The ideological terms that the young militants used to describe their new party rang with the rhetoric of Third World socialism, but the vocabulary and the stated objectives of the party were not foremost in the minds of the Swasa that joined it. They saw it as a way to get out from under the thumb of the Fassi bourgeoisie, to assert themselves in independent Morocco, to be their own men.[8] Still, the Swasa have a habit of resisting established authorities, and the appeal to the common man launched by the UNFP did not fall on deaf ears. It was mostly the retailers that were lured into the UNFP, and Hadj Brahim claims to have followed and not led them. The Soussi big men tried to stay clear of *la boulitique* as they had

[7] But then again commerce is tribal politics by another name. We have come full circle. Attempts to classify social acts in political, religious and economic categories may serve conventional analytic purposes but little more than that. The logic of the layout of this book is that of an American social scientist and not of a Soussi.

[8] A similar phenomenon among the Hausa of Ibadan (Nigeria) has been ably analyzed in Cohen, *Custom and Politics*. He argues that the Hausa have undergone a process of "re-tribalization" as a means to further their own commercial and political interests in the urban context. I would add that the Swasa may have undergone the same process, but without the Hausa's benefits of living in a delineated quarter and having a discernable political structure in the community. The Swasa are scattered throughout the city, and contacts among them are mediated through the distribution system and trips back to the valleys. Despite this dispersion, a general sense of being a Soussi has been generated in the cities, so that one can legitimately speak of "Soussi" communities.

in the violent years prior to 1956. At least initially, however, association with the UNFP did not appear to bear any grave risk, for the King, in 1958 and 1959, had formed a government with a number of ministers known for their sympathy to the new party. This government was to preside over Morocco's first elections of any kind as an independent state, and the Swasa were to play a key role in them.

The "Soussi's revenge" on the Fassi-s was consummated in the elections to the Casablanca Chamber of Commerce and Industry in May, 1960. In the campaign, the ethnic rivalry that motivated the actors—the Swasa to a far greater extent than the Fassi-s—was recast in UNFP rhetoric as the struggle of the progressive wing of the *petite bourgeoisie* against the capitalist oppressors of the *grande bourgeoisie*.

Seats in the Chambers of Commerce of all the major cities were at stake, and the UNFP, not even a year old, ran a slate of candidates against those of the Istiqlal. Once again Ben Barka, now a stalwart of the UNFP, turned to the Swasa for aid. He also reached into the colonial past to resurrect the strategy that the French had tried to apply in 1951, a strategy designed to use Soussi numbers to overwhelm Fassi wealth.

Brahim, as an officer of the Union of Wholesalers and Demi-Wholesalers, helped put together the slate of the UNFP for Casablanca: twenty-four candidates, about half of whom were Soussi. The rest were "Arab" retailers, a few "enlightened" Fassi-s who had cast their lot with the UNFP, and, for balance, two Jews. Among the candidates was Mohammed Mansour. He, like many other resistants, had received a trade license after 1956 as a reward for his sacrifices, and he was thus eligible to run for a seat in the Chamber of Commerce. The slate was obviously pitched to the retail community, to the poor Arabs and Swasa who had always been at the bottom of Casablanca's commercial pile.

The Istiqlal slate, as one might suspect, presented the reverse image. The big names of the Fassi bourgeoisie at Casablanca were all there—Laraqi, Berrada, Ezizzi, Sebti, Bennis, etc.—with a few places left over to faithful Swasa who had never abandoned the party,[9] and to two Jewish candidates.

The electoral procedure, based on the French model, was suitably complicated and presupposed a literate electorate. This fact could have worked against the Swasa and in favor of the educated constituency to which the Istiqlal candidates appealed. Each voter on election day was to be given a list of consecutively numbered names of the candidates. The rub was that there were not only 24 UNFP candidates and 24 Istiqlal candidates, but an additional 67 independents as well. To vote for the men of one's party, the voter had to be able to read their names among 115. He then would draw a line through the names of the twenty-four candidates of his choice and place the ballot in an urn. The regulations stated that if he crossed out as much as one more or less than twenty-four names, the ballot would be voided.

This procedure guaranteed a low turnout in the elections; many retailers, most of whom had never voted before in their lives, could see little point in registering and then picking their way through a maze of regulations to cast their vote. Of Casablanca's 46,000 licensed tradesmen (a higher figure than the previously cited 38,000 because of the inclusion of trades such as barbers and hairdressers), only

[9] Bilqasim Taghawti was the best known Soussi to have remained with Istiqlal after the creation of the UNFP, but not many others were willing to join him.

17,000 registered to vote, and then only 5,800 turned up at the polls. Of those roughly 4,000 made out valid ballots. But that was all the UNFP needed. Brahim and his Soussi allies were able to organize a bigger minority of the commercial community than the Istiqlal. Working with a hard core of about 2,500 tradesmen, the organizers drilled them in electoral procedure and taught them the numbers of the candidates they were to vote for. Memorizing numbers is child's play for Soussi grocers, and they were able to vote for the right candidates even if they could not read their names. The UNFP took every seat in the Casablanca Chamber of Commerce, and did just about as well in several other Moroccan cities. The Swasa had scored their first major victory in urban politics at the expense of their erstwhile mentors from the Istiqlal.[10]

The Istiqlal claimed that the elections had been highly irregular and demanded that they be rerun. The Istiqlal's charges were upheld in court and new elections were scheduled for December, 1960. The UNFP victory in Morocco's first elections had alarmed the King. The UNFP's cautious advocacy of revolution was hardly designed to please the Moroccan theocracy. Immediately following the May elections, Mohammed V swept all the UNFP sympathizers out of his government and let it be known that the party was distinctly *mal-vu*. This may explain in part the sympathy with which the courts received the Istiqlal's complaints of dirty dealings in the UNFP victory.

In December 1960 the two parties went at it again. This

[10] The Swasa were the dominant element in the UNFP victory in elections to the Chambers of Commerce; however, in municipal, local, and parliamentary elections open to universal suffrage the other constituencies of the UNFP came into play: unionized labor, resistants, students, and a smattering of intellectuals, professionals and "enlightened" businessmen.

time the Istiqlal tried to present a slate of "little people." Almost all the Fassi moguls were dropped as candidates, and a number of humble Swasa and Arabs were added. To no avail. The Soussi leaders reactivated their followers and led the UNFP to another resounding victory over the Istiqlal.

But what are we dealing with in these elections: a revolutionary upsurge of downtrodden retailers against the exploiters of the merchant class? Or were Soussi motives less principled? Did they see the UNFP as a suitable vehicle to gain access to the urban patronage system from which they had been excluded by the Fassi bourgeoisie? My own feeling is that both motivations may have been at work but with a clear preponderance of the latter.

"Progressives? Revolutionaries? Yes, well of course I know what the 'intellectuals' in the UNFP have to say about us. Tradesmen think in material terms. They want to better their lot, and that's all. They are realists, and I'm afraid the intellectuals are not. Look, in the Istiqlal we were the poor cousins of the Fassi-s. When Ben Barka and the others created the UNFP for reasons that had nothing to do with us, we had no choice but to join it. For us the Istiqlal meant the Fassi-s, and there was no point in staying with them.[11] But the UNFP began to use us just like the Istiqlal.

"In May, 1960, after the elections, we [the members of the Casablanca Chamber of Commerce] received word that we were all supposed to go over to the Moroccan Union of Labor [Morocco's major industrial labor union, at one time closely affiliated to the UNFP]. Mahjoub Ben Seddiq [the

[11] In conversations a few other Soussi retailers have tended to refute Hadj Brahim's explanation and have laid greater emphasis on their "progressivism and political principles."

head of the union] wanted to tell us how to choose the officers for the Chamber of Commerce. We Soussi-s didn't want to go. How we handled this matter wasn't his business. We didn't give him any advice on workers, and we didn't want any of his advice on commerce. Still we went, and I remember him talking about how the tradesmen exploited the poor, sucking the blood of the workers, etc. We told him that he was way off. Look, we told him, all of the tradesmen give credit in this city. Do you know what would happen if we called in our debts? None of your workers would be able to pay their dues to your union. No one would be able to buy your newspaper that we sell in our shops.

"That is only one of several times that the intellectuals showed their hostility towards us. They always talked about capitalist exploitation, and all I could say was that there are always rich and poor, and there is always commerce, and as long as Morocco was not Communist, these were basic facts.

"So things were bad right from the start with the UNFP. They used us to win in the election, and then the intellectuals began to dictate to us what we should do in the Chamber of Commerce. First Ben Barka and Basri [a former resistance leader] told us we should elect Mohammed Mansour president of the Chamber. Why did they want to do this? Because if the Istiqlal had won, they would have elected Jilali Bennani President, and it was Bennani who had publicly denounced Mansour's bombing of the market in 1953. They wanted to rub it into the Fassi-s, and they wanted to frighten the French business interests in the city, too. So instead of being able to use the Chamber to promote the interests of the retail community, we found ourselves more and more isolated. Following the directives of the party leaders, we made silly demands on the government bcause the UNFP was no longer in it. We talked about nationalizing this and that, and about throwing all the French investors out. We wound up at war with everyone, and the Swasa weren't bettering their sort in the least.

"After two years, in 1962, we were supposed to hold internal elections in the Chamber of Commerce for a new set of officers. It was agreed that the old officers would be re-elected, including myself as treasurer. It was a Friday, and I went to the mosque to pray. When I came back I was in time to hear the nominations read off. My name was omitted, and it turned out that Mansour had arranged to have me eliminated. That didn't bother me much because some of the UNFP leaders later admitted that I had been treated unfairly. But the whole affair was typical of the intellectuals, kowtowing to the resistance, as if we hadn't been in the resistance ourselves."

That same year King Hassan II[12] organized a referendum to approve a constitution that he and his closest collaborators had drawn up themselves. It was Morocco's first constitution and seemingly put some limits upon the King's heretofore undefined powers. Nevertheless the UNFP opposed it on several counts, especially that it was not the product of an elected constituent assembly. The UNFP decided to recommend that its adherents abstain in the referendum. Hadj Brahim found the UNFP tactic misguided and disillusioning. Abstention meant telling people not to go to the polling stations. In the countryside the authorities would be encouraging everybody to show up, and those who absented themselves would be subject to reprisals.

[12] In February 1961 King Mohammed V died and was succeeded by his son Hassan, who has remained on the throne up until the present time.

Brahim felt that UNFP "militants" should go to the polls and vote "No" although that course of action was laden with risk also. Despite his misgivings Brahim agreed to go to Tafrawt and campaign for abstention. In fact 58 percent of the voters at Tafrawt district did abstain, the highest rate for all of Morocco. Brahim noted that Soussi women didn't vote, which may have "inflated the rate a little." In general, however, the UNFP effort was to no avail, and the constitution was overwhelmingly approved.

The constitution provided for a bicameral legislature and elections were scheduled for May, 1963. After having ringingly denounced the constitution, the UNFP decided, about three weeks before the elections, to present candidates for the Chamber of Representatives. Brahim by this time was thoroughly discouraged with the inconsistent behavior of the UNFP, as were many of his Soussi associates at Casablanca. Like several others, he was inclined to keep his distance from the party as the elections approached. A new party had been founded—the Front for the Defense of Constitutional Institutions (FDIC)—that was closely linked to the palace. Not only did the clear support of the King recommend it, but its well-to-do leadership was determinedly anti-Istiqlal, and thus for the Swasa, anti-Fassi as well. FDIC had little trouble in attracting a number of important Swasa (Abdullah Souiri, Hadj Abbid, among others) to its fold. Nonetheless Brahim remained loyal to the UNFP.

It was Mehdi Ben Barka himself who prevailed upon Hadj Brahim to run as the UNFP candidate in the Tafingant district, not far from Tafrawt. Brahim tried to refuse, but Ben Barka told him he owed it to the *khwan* (brothers strictly speaking, but comrades also) in the party. The Hadj reluctantly agreed. He drove down to Tafingant to begin his campaign with his car full of UNFP posters and tracts calling upon the masses to struggle for a socialist future. As soon as he arrived in the valley, he jettisoned his cargo and went about the campaign in his own manner.

"You know, I never mentioned socialism down there. That doesn't mean anything to the people I saw. In fact I ran a very quiet campaign. The qa'id [the local administrator], who was supposed to watch me, didn't know where I was most of the time. There were four other candidates besides myself. There was a FDIC candidate and another one who claimed to be FDIC. There was an Istiqlali who was an 'alim, a neutral candidate, and myself. The other four did what you would expect. They had long luncheons and drank tea with all the big shots who could bring people to the polls. But they were wasting their time. They were winning votes from all sorts of people who couldn't vote at Tafingant because they were registered at Casablanca, or Rabat, or some other big city. Meanwhile I went to work on a couple of tribal fractions whose men still reside in the valley. They are mostly poor peasants, and I reached them through their tulba, who were just as poor. I told them that I wanted to put an end to prostitution and alcoholism and that I wanted to apply Islamic principles. This they could understand.

"So there were no big meals with important people for me. When the qa'id would ask his men 'Where's Hadj Brahim?' they would say, 'He's wasting his time with nobodies.' Both the qa'id and the governor of the province were sure I would lose, and they didn't pay any attention to me. I won by two thousand votes over my nearest opponent."

A political split must have developed in the Soussi community at this point, although it probably did not run very deep. Brahim and some other Swasa were elected to parliament as representatives of the UNFP. They formed what Brahim calls the "popular delegation," as opposed to the other UNFP representatives, who were intellectuals. The whole UNFP parliamentary group amounted to 28 seats, a distinct minority in comparison to the Istiqlal with 41 and FDIC with 69. Still the government must have been surprised and alarmed at the number of UNFP candidates that were elected. The UNFP showing was all the more disquieting in that the legislative elections were to be followed by elections to the Chambers of Commerce, Agriculture and so forth, and it appeared that the UNFP might make considerable gains. These fears may explain the timing of widespread arrests among UNFP leaders, including members of parliament, on accusations of plotting against the King's life. The arrests took place on July 16, just a few weeks before the new round of elections. Hadj Brahim himself was detained thirty-four days, although he was a member of parliament.

The UNFP, as a result of the arrests, had virtually no choice but to boycott the professional Chamber elections, and the Istiqlal did likewise. With a few exceptions, the only candidates in those elections were from FDIC, and they took over all the seats in the various professional chambers. The Casablanca Chamber of Commerce and Industry was still controlled by many of the Swasa who had first been elected under UNFP banners in 1960. They shifted to FDIC in 1963, and Abdullah Souiri became the new President of the Chamber of Commerce. Brahim and Souiri thus found themselves on opposite sides of the political fence, as Brahim and Hadj Abbid had been during the nationalist period. Political antagonisms among the Swasa are handled in the same manner as commercial rivalries. Such divisions are not highly personalized nor emotional and can be easily overcome once the situation that gave rise to them changes.

In the parliament, Brahim once again felt that he and the "popular" representatives were being used by the UNFP intellectuals. The decisions to attack a given governmental policy, to introduce various motions, to vote "No" on a proposed ministerial budget, were taken by the strategists without consultation. Brahim resented the condescension implicit in this treatment.

For example, in 1964, the government without warning nearly doubled the retail price of sugar. They did so to discourage consumption and thus reduce annual sugar imports, which in turn would reduce hard currency purchases of sugar abroad and allow Morocco to rebuild her hard currency reserves. The UNFP seized upon this issue to introduce a censure motion before parliament condemning the government's economic policy. "We weren't really consulted on the advisability of the censure motion, we were just told to vote for it. But then when the intellectuals started to draw up the motion, particularly the sections which showed how brutal the increase in sugar prices was for the average Moroccan, then they found they needed us. We knew about pricing and marketing and consumption habits, and the intellectuals didn't. They had all the brilliant ideas and theories, but we had practical knowledge."

For two years the parliament muddled along. The King was mistrustful of it from the start, and in June, 1965, he dissolved it and declared a state of emergency although nothing very threatening was happening within or without Morocco's borders. Formal political life came to a halt, and Brahim seized the opportunity to drop away from the UNFP. He had fulfilled his obligations to the *khwan*, but there seemed to be little the party could do to further his interests and those of the Swasa in general. The King had asserted himself within the Moroccan political system, bringing to bear the full weight of his administrative and police control of the political process. Association with the opposition became a definite liability, and the "realist" would have to find other means to achieve his ends. The new situation was consecrated when, in 1966, Hadj Brahim was awarded the Ordre du Trone. He thereby received the symbol of political legitimacy and orthodoxy and crossed over the fence that had separated him from some of his colleagues for two years.

Hadj Brahim looked back on his career in the opposition in these terms: "I was always for constructive opposition but not the blind intransigence and opposition for opposition's sake of the UNFP. Right now [1970] there is another constitutional referendum, and the UNFP will vote 'No' again. They should vote 'Yes,' and at least that way they could have some people in parliament and have an audience." I suggested to Hadj Brahim that UNFP leaders would feel they had betrayed their principles if they approved the constitution. "Principles," he snorted. "They can't agree on their principles. The labor unions can't agree with the intellectuals except to say no. In effect they tell the Palace that if we enter the game, you have to leave it. Now obviously that won't work!

"And besides the masses don't understand their principles. They think that if they never compromise some day they will come to power like heroes. But they don't realize one thing. For the masses, angels will become devils as soon as they begin to govern. No, principles and theories aren't enough; there have to be acts. I remember in the parliament one of the intellectuals showed us all sorts of statistics that conclusively proved that in three years the government would be so bankrupt that it wouldn't be able to pay its civil servants. That fatal year has come and gone and the government isn't bankrupt yet. And I don't want it to go bankrupt because that would mean misery for the masses.

"Realism and adaptation are what is needed. Politics is a game, and the players who can't change their ideas can't keep up with the game. There is a verse from the Jahiliya period[13] that says: 'He who has the possibility to do good to others but fails to do so can be left aside and scorned.' The UNFP could have done much good, but has done nothing through its intransigence, and has been left aside."

The transition that Hadj Brahim undertook was away from ostentatious party politics to more acceptable forms of interest group representation as Soussi community spokesman. He had not abandoned *la boulitique*, but the central authorities had laid down new rules to the game to which he was perfectly willing to adapt. "There isn't any political life as before. All that is over now, and perhaps it's for the best."

In the fall of 1966 Hadj Brahim emerged in his new role as a founder and officer of the Moroccan Union of Wholesalers of Food Products (UMGPA). The ceremonies that marked the establishment of the new organization were graced by the presence of a high-ranking official of the Ministry of Commerce. UMGPA has brought within its fold most Soussi tradesmen and wholesalers of consequence, not only in Casablanca but throughout Morocco, as well as numerous other merchants who judged that UMGPA was not only safe but politic to join. UMGPA symbolizes the studious apoliticism of at least the upper reaches of the Soussi community, and their cooperation

---

[13] Pre Islamic Arabic literature and poetry.

with the powers that be. In 1970, when the King offered the country a new constitution and called for a popular referendum to approve or reject it, the UMGPA issued a communiqué stating that its members approved the new text "unreservedly and in its entirety." The year 1962 was obviously best forgotten.

Hadj Brahim could now act as intermediary between his colleagues and the administration, on the one hand to procure for them the benefits and privileges that have been monopolized by the bourgeoisie, and on the other to protect them from administrative red tape and abuse. He is quick to admit that he has been a better protector than provider. The Swasa seem doomed to an inferior role in the urban commercial and patronage system, as an important cog in someone else's grand design.

Typical of Hadj Brahim's function as intermediary was his role in the so-called "retailers' strike" of January, 1969. For reasons that are not entirely clear, the Minister of Finance announced, on December 31, 1968, that the transaction tax would be raised from 8 percent to 12 percent effectively immediately.[14] This is a tax paid by manufacturers and processers, calculated on the price at which they distribute their goods. When the tax hike was announced, the minister declared that absolutely no rise in retail prices would be tolerated. Nonetheless the 4 percent increase was passed down the distribution system from manufacturer (of, say, cooking oil, soap, or beer) to the wholesaler, and finally to the retailer, who in general marked up his prices commensurately. Then on January 27 the Price Control Brigades under the orders of the Ministry of Interior made a sweep—a "razzia" as Hadj Brahim put it—on Casablanca.

[14] Some say that the minister had discovered an unanticipated deficit in the budget and found this a convenient way to fill it.

"They were just soldiers and went from shop to shop. Each time they found an article being sold for more than the price on their lists, they closed the shop. Some people who protested were arrested or beaten."

About two thousand retailers descended on the chamber of commerce to protest these measures. Hadj Brahim, Abdullah Souiri, and others appealed for calm, but also went to work on the city governor and other officials to reconsider the policies being applied. Eventually the authorities agreed to review each case of a shop-closing before pressing any charges. Inspectors went back to the shops to draw up reports, and while they did so the shops remained closed. "This," claims Hadj Brahim, "was what the strike was all about. It was an imposed strike not a voluntary one. Eventually all the charges were dropped against the tradesmen. Prices went up by about 4 percent, and no one interfered. And the Ministry of Finance got its extra revenues."

The political career of Hadj Brahim from 1934 to the present demonstrates his fidelity to his own principles of realism, and adaptability. He has not lost the gift, shared by many of his tribesmates, of a precise sense of power relations and of his own possibilities of action within them. Concomitantly, he and his fellows were in no way stymied by the complexities of national and urban politics, and were able to turn the intricacies of the nationalist and independence periods to their advantage. In this respect, they simply reflected their previously acquired prowess in the commercial sphere.

What has perhaps dominated the Soussi approach to commerce and politics is their fundamental belief in the provisionality of all things and all situations. No victory is definitive, and no loss without recall. No wealth is secure, and no kingdom is eternal. The Soussi attitude toward party politics and particularly their brief role in the opposition is in keeping with their resistance to the French in 1934. They defended their honor but without false heroics. When confronted with overwhelming force, they accommodated themselves to the new order of things. But today, as in 1934, the new order is by no means the final order. Everything on earth is subject to change, and the final order is God's alone.

Chapter VI

◆━━◆━━◆

Islam and
Hadj Brahim's World

IT IS BY now commonplace to characterize Islam as a highly
political religion, perhaps unexcelled in the breadth of its
prescriptions concerning the behavior of man here on earth,
individually and as part of a greater collectivity. The Prophet
Mohammed (d. 632 A.D.) was not only God's voice to man-
kind, speaking the immutable words that became the Koran,
but he and his followers also established, through personal
example, the norms of right conduct that, added to the in-
junctions of the Koran, sustain the various manuals and legal
codes governing the actions of Muslims. Through the Koran,
the *shari'a*, and the *hadith*,[1] the legal underpinnings were laid
down for the constitution of a vast community of believers
(the *umma*) and its political governance. In this community,
all distinguishing traits among believers were to be effaced
in collective "submission" (Islam) to God. Submission to
God would become the glue of a new political community,
superseding existing linkages based on blood, ethnicity,

---

[1] Various compilations of commentary by Muslim scholars on
the deeds and sayings of the Prophet, his companions, and the early
caliphs. These personages are sometimes referred to as the noble
ancestors—*as-salaf as-salih*. Nineteenth and twentieth century reform movements used the term *salafi* to emphasize their return to
the original sources of Islam.

wealth, or language. All men, it was said, stand equal in the eyes of God, and a man can distinguish himself from another only by the degree of his piety and adherence to the tenets of the true faith.

Islamic doctrine was and is, then, not simply political, but, given the basic contours of Middle Eastern society for millenia, revolutionary as well. As a political doctrine, Islam sought to bring under one roof the congeries of tribes, sects, lingual and ethnic minorities, quasi-autarkic cities, and remote villages that had been, through passive or active resistance to central authorities, the undoing of previous political regimes. The Prophet proposed a revolutionary new means of individual identity, that of Muslim, that would, ideally, break down the old barriers to a feeling of oneness and the creation of a homogeneous *umma*. In the new integrated order, the means devised to govern the *umma* were facets of the defense and propagation of the faith and the just application of the *shari'a*. Political and religious authority were one.

Except for brief moments of outward expansion, this religio-political community was never achieved. But as an ideal it has never been abandoned by sincere Muslims, and in some ways is more cherished for the very difficulty of its attainment. Over the centuries, and throughout the Middle East, a tug-of-war, or perhaps better, a dialectic has developed between the bedrock of group particularism and the leveling, homogenizing prescriptions of Islam. Islam, like many political doctrines before and since, has been adopted only to be deformed by its own practitioners. The *umma* exists because there are, clearly, a great many Muslims, but the community has been fragmented by sects and subsects, by rival claims to legitimacy, by the conflict between great and small traditions. Often battles waged in terms of Islamic orthodoxy mask conflicts among lingual and ethnic groups, tribal cleavages, or urban-rural tensions.

Over the centuries, segments of the *umma* have undergone brief moments of reintegration and messianic expansion only to lose the initial *elan* and subside once again into political disintegration. Throughout, the cities have generally preserved and guarded the orthodox traditions. They remain the cultural centers where the original tenets of Islam, and the ideals of right behavior—if not the behavior itself—have been honored. In the countryside—the mountains, the steppe, and the desert—areas more often than not beyond the direct political reach of the cities, tribal and group particularism have been accompanied by animism, fertility cults, and saint worship. These non-Islamic practices have constantly reasserted themselves as part and parcel of the acceleration of centrifugal forces within the *umma*. Sooner or later, the political flabbiness of the regime and the diffusion of decadent practices would evoke the appearance of a religious reformer to urge the community back to the straight path. Like the Prophet before him, the reformer could momentarily rally believers to fight to purge the *umma* of incompetent leaders and evil habits. But, if successful, within a generation or so the centrifugal forces would once again take command, preparing the ground for yet another reform movement.[2] James Siegel, writing about Islam in western Sumatra, has stated the essential dilemma of Islamic integration nicely:[3]

[2] This analysis is, of course, borrowed directly from Ibn Khaldoun. It has been rephrased and amplified by Ernest Gellner, "Pendulum Swing Theory of Islam," in Roland Robertson, ed., *Sociology of Religion* (Baltimore, 1969), pp. 127–128.

[3] James T. Siegel, *The Rope of God* (Berkeley and Los Angeles: University of California Press, 1969), p. 67.

...so long as kinship and locality were the bases of social organization, reform movements could not succeed in making Islamic law, as the ulema conceived it, the basis of social life in any permanent way. The appeal of these movements was not the reform of social life, but the dissolution of traditional and social bonds in favor of another, albeit temporary, kind of identity.

The history of Morocco as a Muslim society can be interpreted within the terms presented above. Islam was introduced into Morocco between 647 and 710 A.D., at a time when the society was almost exclusively Berber. Although the indigenous population gradually and overwhelmingly adopted the new religion, nonurban Moroccans have always experienced some anxiety as to their status as "good Muslims." They did not speak the language of the Prophet and the Koran; they were not Arabs, the people chosen by God to spread the faith; and the Arabs argued that the Berbers did not adopt the faith spontaneously, but as a conquered people.[4] The implication has been that the Berber is a second class Muslim. Ironically, the French in Morocco favored just this line in their attempt to convince the Berbers to cast off Islam entirely. The attempt backfired, and many Berbers redoubled their effort to assert their Muslim identity. Some did so, most recently, by adhering to the reform movement of the twentieth century, one that amalgamated Islamic reform and national liberation. Those Berbers that participated in it, like Hadj Brahim, underscored their religious orthodoxy as well as their national identity.

As was noted in Chapter III, the French became aware early on that the Soussi *tulba* and *ulema*, those Swasa whose

[4] A good history of Morocco is Jean Brignon et al., *Histoire du Maroc* (Casablanca, 1967). On the Muslim conquest, see pp. 46–57.

cultural ties with Arabic and Islam were most developed, were the principal spokesmen for the nationalist movement in the Anti-Atlas. In this context, as nationalists and Muslims, the Swasa could lay claim to their own legitimacy and dignity vis à vis the literate Arab Muslims of the cities. Hadj Brahim pointed out to me that the Chleuh often acted as guardians of the faith when the cities had fallen into decadence. Ibn Toumert (d. 1128 A.D.) whose crusade to purify Moroccan Islam led to the founding of the Almohades Dynasty (al-Muwahhidun), was a Soussi from the Anti-Atlas. Resistance to the Portuguese, who set up a string of settlements along the Atlantic coast in the fifteenth and sixteenth centuries, was also most virulent in the mountains of the south. Hadj Brahim is prepared to argue that the "real" Moroccans, the "real" Muslims of Morocco, are by no means all concentrated in the northern cities. The Sous has its own great traditions and sources of Islamic pride. Brahim emphatically denies a special role for the Arabs in Islamic traditions. "Islam is not Arab; everyone knows that. Only the ignorant and the chauvinists try to build the Arabs into something they are not. One has only to look at the companions of the Prophet to know the truth. There was Belal the Habbashi [the Ethiopian], a black man and a slave. There was Soulaib the Rumi [the Greek] and Salman the Farissi [the Persian]. These were his followers when his uncle remained an infidel."

Hadj Brahim will concede to no Muslim, Arab or otherwise, in the "quality" of his piety. He is self-consciously orthodox in his interpretation of Islam (a self-proclaimed adherent to the Salafi reform movement, of which more later), and he has obviously thought deeply about his identity as a Muslim. Clifford Geertz sees this conscious self-affirmation as Muslims as typical of Moroccans in the twentieth century. He argues that, faced with subordination to the Christian power of France, the individual Moroccan's identity as Muslim became a matter of personal policy rather than a predictable, and unquestioned, circumstance of one's birth.[5] But Geertz may be overlooking the fact that his "oppositional Muslims" are an old phenomenon closely linked to Moroccans' doubts regarding their claims to Muslim-ness, doubts arising, in part, because of their physical and spiritual status as a fringe population on the outer edge of the great centers of Islamic learning in the Arab East. Hadj Brahim is an "oppositional Muslim," but not so much in reaction to the French as in reaction to the Fassi-s, the self-proclaimed defenders of Arabdom and the Prophet's way in the land of the Berbers. Hadj Brahim, through his espousal of Salafi reform, not only meets the Fassi-s on their own ground of orthodoxy but shows that as a Berber he is as much a Muslim as any one of them.

It would be simplistic to suggest that Hadj Brahim's faith is no more than an ideological device to aid him in identifying himself within the Islamic cultural tradition of Morocco. Above all else, he believes profoundly in Allah and the correctness of His prescriptions as embodied in the Koran. This faith in and comprehension of God's will is independent of the fact that he is a Berber. From his understanding, he draws the perspectives that enable him to interpret the vast array of human experience which he has witnessed. It provides him with a logic to order his own priorities and to determine the causes of success and failure.

Moreover, it seems to me, that Hadj Brahim's faith helps him make sense of the rapid changes he and most other Moroccans have undergone in this century. Provisionality has

[5] Clifford Geertz, *Islam Observed: Religious Development in Morocco and Indonesia* (Yale University Press, 1968), p. 65.

been a salient feature of Moroccan political and economic systems in recent decades. Hadj Brahim assumes the fragility of human relations and inconsistency of human roles and seeks the predictability and consistency that would otherwise be lacking in his life in Islam.

Hadj Brahim's life, and his interpretation of it, are testimony to his ability to thrive in what we would call inconsistent, at times incongruous, situations. Such situations appear to place no particular stress upon Hadj Brahim. He regards them as normal, as do most of his countrymen. His ability to operate with "others" simultaneously at several levels of friendship and animosity, is a direct affront to our craving for certainty.[6] Westerners treating with the Hadj Brahims of numerous countries are wont to talk of the perfidiousness, or double-dealing, of the natives. These Westerners expect relations established today to be valid and predictable years from now. They are not attuned to the *situational* changes that bring about realignments and adjustments in these relationships. It is a bit like the Lone Ranger and Tonto surrounded by Apaches. "This looks like it, Tonto; we'll go down together," intones the Lone Ranger. To which Tonto replies, "What you mean 'we,' White Man?"[7]

[6] The psychological need for consistency in conflict-relations in American society is developed by J. S. Coleman in *Community Conflict* (Free Press, 1956). Leon Festinger has analyzed how people cope with conflicts between acts and norms. However, Festinger is clearly aware that "cognitive dissonance" is a phenomenon relative to the varying norms of differing societies. "The dissonance exists simply because the culture defines what is consonant and what is not. In some other culture these two cognitions might not be dissonant at all." *A Theory of Cognitive Dissonance* (Row, Peterson, 1957), p. 14.

[7] Rokeach notes that most American studies of attitudes deal with attitudes towards *objects*: for instance, attitudes towards

The West has an obsession with undying friendships and eternal alliances, unconditional surrenders, fighting to the last man, and establishing lasting peace. Hadj Brahim marvels at our naiveté. In his eyes we deny the very essence of human affairs, their provisionality. "Unconditional surrender? Just look at Germany and Japan today. Everybody has his day in the sun, but just for a little while." We in the West fly in the face of the logic God has built into His world, and it is we, rather than those who believe in the one God, who are fanatics.

Without his belief in the one God, Hadj Brahim might well succumb to the anxiety generated by the ambiguous situations through which he must propel himself. But this world is not his only frame of reference, and he is not driven to make a lasting mark upon it. Not that he lacks a craving for certainty and clarity, but he has found both in Islam. For Hadj Brahim belief in Islam not only sustains him as he copes with his existence, but, insofar as it is *reasoned* belief more than faith, it explains all that he must bear in this world. Islam, as propounded by Hadj Brahim, is a logical system, all of whose parts mesh perfectly, all of whose workings can be *understood*. When he talks about his religion, he is serene

blacks, candidates, or breakfast foods. Little attention has been paid to attitudes towards *situations*—that is, the black who wants to buy a white's house—and how the two sets of attitudes interact. Studying such attitudinal interaction rigorously may allow us to discover consistency in what appears at first to be inconsistent behavior. See Milton Rokeach, "Attitude Change and Behavioral Change," *Public Opinion Quarterly*, XXX, 4 (Winter 1966–1967), 529–550. James Mosel has confronted the same phenomenon in Thailand. He approaches it from the point of marginal involvement in roles so that contradictory roles produce little psychic stress. See his "Communication Patterns and Political Socialization in Transitional Thailand," in Lucien Pye, ed., *Communications and Political Development* (Princeton University Press, 1967), pp. 184–228.

yet somewhat combative. He wants to communicate the beauty and the security that he sees in its logic. He wants his listener to test it and challenge it with specific problems.

Brahim exists in two worlds; the ambiguous and pro-visional secular world and the logically infallible world of God. However, it is not that he exists in one *or* the other; he exists in both. The secular is made palatable and is explained by the religious, and each secular act has significance in the world of God. Islam allows Brahim to make the best of both worlds.[8]

Not only is Islam a comfort to Hadj Brahim in a funda-mentally unpredictable world, but in addition Islam explains that the world is ever thus. It does so through insistence upon two interrelated themes: the notion of paired opposites and the notion of a cyclical process in human events. The first notion is summed up by Hadj Brahim by the axiom "Every-thing comes in pairs." It forewarns man that he can never have it all one way, that he must know failure as well as success, poverty as well as plenty. He who would try to escape this inexorable law is simply arrogant and impious in the eyes of God. The notion of cyclical processes rein-forces the belief in the provisionality of all situations and at the same time encourages individuals and societies to submit

[8] Kenneth Brown, commenting on my analysis, expressed his reservations in terms that warrant full reproduction here: "The ambiguity of the 'real' and certainly of the 'eternal' is not, to my mind, a satisfactory explanation of Hadj Brahim's world. His ideology and polemics serve some function, especially in a dialogue with a Christian. But even a Christian polemicist, or a Jew, would make something of the same argument. . . . The difference is, I think, that Hadj Brahim's faith is whole, that his world is one, that the kind of moral questions that lead to anxiety in the West simply do not exist. . . ." Letter of 28/3/71.

patiently to those situations. Sooner or later they will come full circle; those up will be down, the vanquished will become victor. No situation is hopeless, for no situation is permanent.

"Everything is paired, everything comes in two's. Every man must suffer physically and psychologically. You asked me about losing four children. Of course it was hard. I buried each one. But all that is part of my share of hardship, and there was nothing for me to do but carry on. For every man there is happiness and sadness, poverty and wealth, sickness and health. We all experience rest and fatigue, hot and cold, ignorance and knowledge. Even electricity confirms the rule with positive and negative currents. There is never any one of these things without the other.

"Look at the question of wealth. Every man craves wealth, money and goods. But it is a silly craving that can never be satisfied. Islam lets us try to gain as much as we can in our lifetimes but then obliges us to divide it all up among our heirs when we die. They have to start from zero. Accumulating wealth is an illusion, all grandeur is temporary.

"There will always be divergence among men as long as the world exists. Even the family is divided; harmony and divergence come together. In the Spanish Civil War families were divided, and brothers killed each other. Today the Communists who want to establish a universal order are divided among themselves. They think that it is temporary, but that is the way it always is.

"And all this talk about peace. Has man ever lived in peace? Is there less war now than before? There will be periods of peace, but there will always be war. Here is the modern era, and man has the technological capacity for the first time in history to feed everybody. He also has the technological capacity to destroy everybody. Even that is paired.

"I always say that there are many religions but no religious people. There is Judaism, Christianity and Islam, but where are the Jews, the Christians and the Muslims? All religions preach the fraternity of man and nonviolence. But fraternity and nonviolence exist nowhere. Maybe God meant us to be incapable of practicing our own religions. One thing is sure, however; a bad Muslim or a bad Jew is better than an atheist who rejects the true as well as the false.

"So there we are with evil and good, those who follow the straight path and those who deviate. There is never one without the other. It is like the body; we have two hands, two eyes, two feet. Everything comes in two's except one thing, the heart. For when a man has been good in his life, God takes his heart; but if he has been evil his heart goes to Satan. For, you see, while all is paired on earth, God alone is unpaired. There are not two Gods. He has no associate, no Holy Ghosts. He is one, undivided, unique. Unity is found only in God.

"All of God's good creations are rare. There are more flies than bees, more wild animals than domesticated animals, more weeds than flowers. So it is with religious men. They are very few. A man without religion is an animal, no more than a donkey. Unfortunately there are more donkeys than men."

Hadj Brahim is deeply interested in the two other religions Islam enjoins its followers to respect. Christians and Jews, according to the Koran, are people of the book (*ahl al-kitab*), and their scriptures and religious beliefs are sacred to Muslims. Hadj Brahim's understanding of the monotheistic religions is at times simplistic, perhaps reflecting his tacit conviction that they are but evolutionary stages leading to Islam.

"Those who know religion and understand it will never

combat it. And those who do not believe in *all* the prophets believe in nobody. I've read all the great books, the Old Testament and the New Testament, and I still know the Koran by heart. These are the three true religions. And what counts in all of them is above all the spirit, and only secondarily the rites. Beliefs first and then acts.

"We must believe in all the prophets, and, indeed, each prophet said another would follow him and that the successor must be honored. The only continuity in the chain of prophets was the fundamental belief in the unity of God. The Middle East is the oldest civilization of the world and has produced the most prophets. It is the original source of progress and intelligence in the world.

"Each prophet performed miracles to prove his authenticity. Each suited his miracles to the epoch in which he lived. He had to adapt them to the customs of the people to whom he was sent. For example Moses was sent to the Egyptians, and the pharaohs were always surrounded by magicians. So Moses struggled with the magicians on their own terms by turning sticks into snakes and so forth. Now Christ came at the time that the Romans were powerful, and the Romans were interested in everything medical. Great progress was made in medicine at that time. Thus Christ worked miracles of healing, raising the dead, giving sight to the blind, and curing cripples. The Prophet Muhammad was sent to the Arabs. Everyone knows that the Arabs have always been impassioned by literature and poetry. Muhammad's miracle—his only miracle—was to receive the Koran from God. The Prophet was totally illiterate, yet the text he recited is flawless; it is immutable. In it he describes the sea perfectly although he had never seen it, and many other such things, proving that it was God-given. None of the greatest Arabic scholars have ever found an error in it. It is the same unchangeable text for all Muslims. There is no King James version of the Koran. That is the Prophet's miracle.[9]

"None of the prophets was ever followed by a majority of the people to whom he was sent. Above all, they were never followed by the rich. The rich would always say, 'Why did God choose that vagabond and not me?' So the prophets had only the poor and the slaves, like Moses with the Jews of Egypt. Most of the prophets were old too. Only Christ and John were called before they were forty. They always came alone, and it had to be that way. If a prophet came supported by his tribe, no one would believe that he was a prophet. They would believe that he was just another ambitious pretender. Muhammad was not supported by his own tribe, Quraish. That proved that he relied on God alone.

"Muhammad is the last of the prophets, and so it is written in the Koran. But why is this? It took centuries, but man is now mature, intellectually and morally. There is no more need for prophets. Man creates his own miracles with technology. Could you imagine a man today who presents himself as a prophet? Our customs won't tolerate such things any more. There will be no more prophets.

"Judaism is the oldest religion. The Prophet Abraham led the children of Israel. Moses was sent by God, a divine ambassador. But the Jews refuse to recognize any of the prophets that came after Moses. That's the major divergence between Judaism and Islam. The Jews discriminate among the prophets. And the Christians say that they killed Christ,

[9] According to Hadj Brahim, the Shi'is, a dissident branch of Islam who believe that the sons of Ali should have succeeded to the Caliphate, also believe that when the Angel Gabriel gave the Koran to Muhammad, he did so in error, for it was actually intended for Ali.

the Son of God, and that's why there is divergence between Christians and Jews. There is never anything illogical in any of the sacred texts, and Christ said that one day a man sent by God would come and that he must be followed. Christ meant Muhammad. The Jews deny all that; they deny the truth.

"The Jews are the oldest people on earth, and Judaism is the oldest religion. But fortunately God did not want them to be numerous. That is why a person can be Jewish only if his mother is Jewish. If it were otherwise, the Jews would be as numerous as the Chinese. It is easy to have a father; he could marry several women, including non-Jews. He could adopt many children and make them Jews. But for women all that is far more difficult.

"As for Christianity, Muslims cannot accept the claim that Christ is the son of God. It is denied in the Koran. Christians talk about the miracle of the virgin birth. If Christ's birth is a miracle, then think about the birth of Adam who had neither father nor mother. All this is ridiculous. If God had a son, then God himself must have had a father and mother, no?

"And there is the question of the crucifixion and the death of Christ. Now if Christ was the son of God, it is impossible to believe that God would have let him be killed. No parents will ever let their children be killed—it's illogical. If Christ was killed against God's will, then he is no longer a God, but a coward.

"Anyone who has to eat and drink and die is a man. Christ was a man.

"According to the Koran, Christ is not dead. Another man who looked like him was crucified in his place. There is no tomb for Christ. However, Christ will die eventually.

Everyone dies eventually, even the angels. Satan and Gabriel will die.

"The angels are without number and without sex. They obey absolutely the will of God, and they are sinless. Yet there are great and small angels, and some are better than others. That is the way it is for all the creatures of God. Gabriel is one of the four great angels. He is the judge of the angels themselves. Mikhail is the angel of well-being. Israfil is the trumpeter for the end of the first day and the beginning of the second day of judgment. Azrail is the angel of death. Every living being is in his hands. Satan of course rules in hell. He refused to accept the goodness of Adam who was created out of clay while Satan himself was created out of lightning. God threw Satan out of paradise but gave him a reprieve. As long as man, the sons of Adam, lives on earth, Satan will live, but he will die when man dies. Satan can harm no one who is firmly attached to God; but he will always try out of hatred for the sons of Adam who caused him to be thrown out of heaven."

Hadj Brahim's interpretation of Islam is strict; to call it puritan does not seem out of place. He works out the ramifications of his beliefs around the overriding theme of the unity of God, His unique and indivisible nature. This tenet has as its logical counterpart the absolute equality of all God's creatures. The inequalities that living creatures must endure are of little consequence on that day when all stand naked before their Creator.

"You will confront God without anyone's aid. On that day each man is utterly alone. In the final reckoning blood counts for nothing; brothers count for nothing; ancestors count for nothing. The Prophet himself told his family, his own wife, that on the day of judgment there would be nothing that he could do for them, that they would all stand alone. Even the Prophet's uncle, Abu Talib, who had helped him, could not be saved by Muhammad. Abu Talib died an infidel and stood alone in the eyes of God."

Hadj Brahim places himself emphatically in the Salafi tradition of Islam, which seeks to cleanse the Muslim community of heterodox practices, such as saint worship, and restore it to the pure tradition of the first caliphs. In this respect, the Hadj is unusual among the Swasa who, like many other Moroccans, are given to various brotherhoods and orders founded to carry on the rites of a renowned saint.[10] He is aware that his beliefs are not completely attuned to those of his community, and he does not mince words in deploring the aberrant forms of Islam that his fellows have adopted. It is the question of intermediaries between God and man, the notion that there is a hierarchy of God's creatures, that most annoys him. From the elaborate ritual of the orders to a simple prayer at a saint's tomb, the tradition of saint worship is predicated upon the efficacy of intercession of the "elect" between God and man. But, as Hadj Brahim sees it, there is and can be no "elect" among the community of believers, no groups of men who have special access to God's grace. Those that lay claim to powers of intercession bring false comfort to the ignorant and the afraid but do not advance them one step towards piety and salvation.

"There can be no intermediaries between God and man. There are no saints on the day of judgment. No one knows

[10] See, for instance, Emile Dermenghem, *Le Culte des Saints dans l'Islam maghrebin* (Paris: Gallimard, 1954). For the political functions of saints and their descendants, see Ernest Gellner, *Saints of the Atlas*, (London: Weidenfeld and Nicolson, 1969).

what God will do on that day. Those who pretend that they can intercede are not part of Islam. *Moussems* [annual pilgrimages to saints' tombs], saints, even the sacred places [Mecca, Medina], that's not religion. The *shurfa* [descendants of the Prophet] and their *baraka* [the power to bless and bring well-being attributed to *shurfa*]—none of that is part of religion. Muhammad himself could bestow no *baraka*, so how is it that his descendants can?[11]

"No one knows God's will; no one can predict the future. You say that in a couple of hours you will get in your car and drive to Rabat. That, you say, you can predict. But do you know what you will see on the road? In fact we know very little, and it is our pride that makes us think we know a lot. When a man who has succeeded in business says, 'It's thanks to Sidi Ahmed ou Moussa [a saint of the Tazeroualt] that I did well,' that is a sin. And if a man says, 'It's thanks to my efforts alone,' that is worse yet. There are no associates in God's will. It is always thanks to God's will alone.

"It's incredible the nonsense people believe in. All these saints and magicians that the women go to—it's terrible. People say that such and such a saint leapt from mountain top to mountain top or flew to Damascus in a twinkling of an eye. But how can they believe that when the Prophet Muhammad, the beloved of God, had to walk ten days to go from Mecca to Medina?

"You know, many Europeans have converted to Islam because they realize that their religion denies the unity of God and thus denies equality among men. I can remember at Tangier that Catholic women could go to a priest and pay

[11] Morocco's ruling dynasty is composed of *shurfa* descended from the Prophet, and many Moroccans believe that their rulers have *al-baraka*.

him two *pesetas* to have permission to eat meat on Fridays. Now really, am I supposed to believe that a poor priest for a couple of pennies can relieve someone of a sacred obligation? Someone told me about a Dutchman who was going to Cairo to study. Before leaving, his parents took him to church so that he could confess. The priest pardoned his sins, and off he went. At Cairo he began to study the Koran. He kept reading over and over again that the Prophet Abraham, beloved of God, continually prayed that God would pardon his sins. The Dutchman realized that if Abraham had to pray to God that his sins be pardoned, then it is ridiculous to suppose that a priest could pardon the sins of a lesser man. The Dutchman converted to Islam.

"As I said before, there is Islam but very few Muslims. I think the true Muslims are the Salafists. I have read all the works of Abduh and Afghani, and also the writings of the great *shaikh* al-Alawi,[12] and all the books of Mokhtar as-Soussi, although he was a Darqawi [one of the major religious orders in North Africa]. There is nothing to equal the *Sahih* of al Bukhari.[13] He presents only the surest traditions [*hadith*] of the Prophet, those about which there can be no dispute. He records four thousand *hadith* filtered in the light of the wisdom of the greatest scholars of Islam. Bukhari does not try to overwhelm you with huge numbers of traditions, many of which may be false. He practices one of our proverbs: 'Too much of something is a loss' ['*ziyyada fishay naqsa*']."

In Hadj Brahim's discussion of Islam there is an undeniable element of fatalism centered on the futility of hu-

---

[12] A famous Moroccan Salafi reformer and nationalist who died in 1965.

[13] A particularly famous collection of sayings and deeds attributed to the Prophet and his companions.

man efforts in the face of the inscrutability of God's will. Throughout much of the literature dealing with the Middle East in general and Morocco in particular, the inertia that various observers discern in the traditional or peasant society is attributed to religious fatalism. Moroccans themselves are wont to shrug off situations that they cannot control with the simple phrase "it is written" (*maktub*).[14] Quite clearly, however, Hadj Brahim has never acted as if all was beyond his control. He does not passively submit to his fate; rather he actively submits to his fate.

"Monsieur, there are three chapters to Islam, and this is the very essence of religion. Those chapters are faith, religious obligations, and liberty. All Muslims agree on these chapters. Let me explain those chapters to you. First there is faith and belief. This consists of belief in the one God, belief in the angels, and belief in all the prophets, Muhammad being the last, the seal of the prophets. It means that the Muslim believes in all the holy books and in the day of judgment. We believe that when the second trumpet sounds all the dead will arise in a single place. Each will be given a book in which all his acts have been recorded, and he will be able to read it even if he is illiterate. There is a bridge over Hell as narrow as a hair that all will have to cross. Some will cross it, and others will fall. Of course none of this is literal; we can't know how the final judgment will be.

"The second chapter are our obligations as Muslims, the rituals of Islam. There is no disagreement on these. We all perform five prayers each day, and not seven or ten. We fast during the month of Ramadan, we pay alms [*zakat*], and if possible we make the pilgrimage to the Holy Places. Now

[14] *Maktub* may be an artifact of Western ethnography. As Ken Brown pointed out to me, a Moroccan is more likely to say "That which is" *dak shi lli kayn*.

finally there is the chapter of liberty. God has placed only three limitations on what we can do in this world. We must not infringe upon the liberties of others; we must not take the property of others; and we must not say anything untrue or insulting about others. If you honor these three rules then you can do whatever you want. It is for this chapter that God gave us all a soul. Animals don't have souls, only man. And we have to have it because we can do good or evil. Only we have the power of choice, the choice to do right or wrong, and on the day of judgment we will answer for the choices we have made. This is what the third chapter is all about. God knows each and every choice that we have made. There is no way to hide our choices although we may try. In the Sous we say that whatever a man does in hiding is a sin. [15]

"We are not helpless, and we make choices to try to better ourselves. When you hear people talking about *maktub*, what this really means is that everything that is done is done with the knowledge and consent of God. What is written always has a cause, and we know that cause. He who does not sow will not reap. *Maktub* means that we can do absolutely nothing *against* the will of God, but that we are capable of everything with His will.

"So you see it is not Islam that ties us down. Really the problem is discipline. It takes discipline to work hard. In the

[15] Brahim seems to be following a schema that Siegel discerned in Sumatra. There it is believed that man's nature has two parts: his *hawa nafsu* or desire, passion, and egoism; and his *aqal* or powers of reason. Adam was thrown from paradise for giving in to his *hawa nafsu*; but his descendants, through their *aqal*, can *understand* God's commands and find their way back to paradise. But no good can come from *aqal* unless it is guided by religion. Siegel, *Rope of God*, pp. 101–104.

great age of Islam our religion provided that discipline. And it still does to the extent that there are Muslims who practice it. Religion is very practical and necessary in that sense. In the countryside, it is not the police who keep order but religion. In the cities if a man is drunk or a woman indecent, it is not the police who prevent immorality. Good Muslims prevent it themselves. But this social discipline is dwindling, what with the youth and the hippies and our attachment to world civilization. And as it dwindles we are capable of less and less.

"I'll admit that religions like anything else can cause excesses. I've been out to India, China, Formosa, and Japan a few times to buy tea. In Calcutta they throw the garbage in the streets. Then the crows come every morning to feed on it. And then the cows finish what the crows have left. That's their garbage collection system. All that good beafsteak running around and nobody can eat it. They do that in the name of religion.

"But people who are concerned by our society should hope to see religion reinforced, not diminished. Islam provides all that is necessary for social harmony. Just look at the system of alms. The *shari'a* says that a man must pay 2 ½ percent of his monetary worth in alms each year. He must also pay 10 percent [*'ashur*] of his agricultural produce. He can pay less on his money because no one sees it,[16] but everyone can see his grain and his trees. So these taxes contain social revolution and keep order.

"In the Sous, before the French came, the collection of *'ashur* was very important. Every year what was collected would be divided in thirds. One third went to the poor, one

[16] Cf. Hadj Brahim's remark that what a man does in hiding is a sin.

third to the *madersa*-s to feed the students, and the last third to al-Hiba.[17] After the French came, the *'ashur* was divided evenly between the poor and the *madersa*-s.

"After independence Mukhtar Soussi wanted to establish a college in the Sous to train Swasa in theology and *shari'a*. He called on Hadj Abbid, Ahmed Oulhadj and others to help find money for it. We worked out an agreement with King Mohammed V to found the Islamic Institute of Taroudant. It gave courses in modern subjects as well as religion, and students could study French there. We set up branches at Massa, Ait Baha, and Sidi Bibi, and at Taroudant alone there were two thousand students, all of whom were boarders. Between 1958 and 1963 the *'ashur* collected in the region went one-third to the poor, one-third to the *madersa*-s, and one-third to the Institute. This was all done locally and according to Islamic taxes. Then in 1963 the governor of Agadir province refused to allow the *'ashur* to be collected, and it has never been collected since. The state took over the Institute and it is now known as the Institute Mohammed V. It is run like a regular state *lycée*. But you can see that operating within the Islamic framework we were able to do a great deal; we were in no way held back by our fatalism and traditionalism.

"If only we all understood our religion, then we could meet the modern world with serenity. Our problem is not too much religion but too little, and what there is is misunderstood. You asked me what it was like to make the pilgrimage to Mecca and Medina. Well I know lots and lots of Hadj-s who have gone for the prestige, so that they can have

[17] Al-Hiba, in 1910, was proclaimed Sultan by Soussi *ulema*, and in 1912 he crossed the Atlas and seized the city of Marrakesh. Shortly thereafter he was defeated in the field by a French force, outside of Marrakesh.

Hadj in front of their name and so that people will treat them with respect. But that is not the purpose of the Hadj. The Hadj is a religious obligation to be undertaken in all humility, and that is why I went. The others have perverted their obligation. It is said that the Kaaba stone is the first construction on earth, the first stone placed by man. It is there that we confirm ourselves as the sons of Adam, the creatures of God. Yet many go to raise themselves above their fellow men.

"When I went to Mecca I wanted to learn, for the Koran tells us to search for knowledge even if it be in China. (I've learned a few things there too.) On my way to Mecca I visited Frankfurt, Munich, Istanbul, Ankara, Adana, Nicosia, Beirut, Damascus, Aleppo, Hams, Amman, Jerusalem, Hebron, and Bethlehem. All that was in the spring of 1962. Islam gave us the pilgrimage so that we could learn about one another, and I wanted to profit from that. [18]

"I visited the refugee camps too, and it was awful. Having seen that, anyone could understand what is happening now. Both sides have to compromise, but everyone forgot about the Palestinians. They were left out of all the calculations. Now everyone is talking about the refugees, but there are no refugees, only Palestinians. One day disaster is going to befall King Hussein. And Nasser has as little room for

[18] I had expected that recounting his own pilgrimage, what I assumed to be his quintessential act as a Muslim, would trigger off some deep probing into his own sense of religious identity. I was mistaken, and he treated this event as matter-of-factly as most of the others we had discussed. There was a familiar note of detachment in his narrative, as if he were stepping back a few paces to look at himself in action. This detachment may have been a manifestation of his reluctance to let down his guard in front of a Christian. For instance, he never probed me too deeply into the nature of my own religious beliefs, perhaps out of fear of what he would find.

manoeuvre as the Jews. He too has his back to the sea, his own population, which will sweep him away if he doesn't resist.

"I wonder if maybe the Oriental Jews can change Israel. You know they are terribly discriminated against by the European Jews. The European Jews control everything in the government and the economy, but it's thanks to the Oriental Jews that Israel was able to colonize so much land. I've always thought that inside Israel it's just like the Fassi-s and us. The European Jews are the Fassi's and the Oriental Jews, the Swasa."

Hadj Brahim flatly declared, "If there had been any real Muslims, we would never have been beaten by the Israelis." I noted that according to his general appreciation, there probably were not many real Jews either, so that on that score Muslims and Jews were evenly matched. The Hadj, for once, seemed slightly nonplussed. "Yes, that's true. Who knows how the Jews won? The Jews themselves were practically exterminated twice by the Babylonians, and yet the Babylonians had no religion at all. I suppose that these victories represent nothing. Where is Babylon today?

"What I can't understand is the attitude of the Europeans. They attack us for our religion and our so-called fanaticism. I am convinced that European racism towards the Arabs is really religious hatred. The Muslims were Europe's last great enemy before the industrial revolution, and once they achieved the technological edge, they have taken it out on us ever since. Why, just look at Biafra. All of Europe was defending the Ibo-s against the northern Muslims. Yet at the same time the Europeans couldn't care less what happens to the Vietnamese—except if they are Catholic Vietnamese.

"When I look at the future all I can see is confusion. Our people are adrift; they don't understand their own values. On the one hand, the young abandon all their principles, and on the other, the traditionalists feel that all can be put right by a blind imposition of rigid rules. No wonder that our societies have gone astray! Islam is great precisely because it is not a tradition. It does not say that what our elders have done is necessarily good for us. The most traditional Muslims are the most ignorant. They become obsessed by what is unimportant. Neither clothes nor haircuts are religion. How can we face real problems when Muslims worry about mini-skirts?

"I cannot blame Europeans for not understanding Islam when so few Muslims understand it. This has been a problem for Islam from the beginning. The simple-minded want easy solutions and magic. They don't realize that there is no magic, that everything has a cause and can be explained. That is the real magic, the rationality of God's universe. Bukhari recounts that at the time the Prophet went to Medina, a bedouin went to visit him at his camp. The bedouin was prepared to believe anything and probably wanted the Prophet to perform a few miracles. He rode up on his camel outside the praying grounds and was greeted by the Prophet, who invited him to prayer. The bedouin asked him if he should tie up his camel or count on God to keep the beast from wandering off. The Prophet said, 'Count on God, and tie up your camel.' "

Chapter VII

The Reification of Hadj Brahim and the Swasa

To reduce something unknown to something known, soothes and tranquilizes one's mind, and in addition produces a feeling of power. The first principle: any explanation is better than no explanation at all. Inasmuch as it is a question of ridding oneself of disquieting phenomena, one does not look too closely in grasping the means to do so; the first interpretation by which the unknown becomes known is so reassuring that it must be true.

PIERRE BOURDIEU, ET.AL.[1]

IN THIS chapter I shall impose a partial analytic order upon the Swasa to make "sense" of their transformation, and to place them in the Western social scientists' understanding of economic change and growth. I am not convinced that my treatment will be fair nor that I have the data base to justify the generalizations that follow. Moreover, although Hadj Brahim would understand the hypotheses we apply to him, he would probably find them irrelevant to what he feels are

[1] Pierre Bourdieu, et.al., *Le Métier de Sociologue: Livre I* (Paris: Mouton, 1968), p. 49.

the essentials of his life and those of his fellow Swasa. Nonetheless my attempt is warranted, for the economic development of the Third World is a matter of legitimate concern to social scientists, and they will seek to place the Hadj Brahims of that world in some analytic framework whether or not their tools of analysis are up to the task.

My own discussion breaks down into two parts: the nature of the market and exchange system in which the Swasa operate; and the way in which their experience is important to theories of achievement motivation. To sustain some of my points, I draw on evidence from earlier chapters, but the interpretations and explicit normative judgments that I make are my own and not, as will probably be obvious, Hadj Brahim's.

THE BAZAAR ECONOMY

In his careful study of merchants in a middle-sized Javanese town, Clifford Geertz has extrapolated the mechanisms of distribution and exchange in the increasingly integrated market economy of contemporary Indonesia. Taken together these mechanisms constitute a model of what Geertz calls the bazaar (*pasar*) economy.[2] The Modjokuto trading community and the Swasa of Casablanca share many features, but some fundamental differences are indicated by the very use of the term "bazaar" to characterize the system Geertz has under scrutiny. The bazaar patterns of Modjokuto date back at least to the fourteenth century, and the traders themselves, coming from a long tradition of preindustrial traders, see themselves, like the Fassi-s, as the

[2] Geertz, *Peddlers and Princes*, esp. Chapter 3, "Economic Development in Modjokuto," pp. 28–81.

standard bearers of moral excellence and culture in their society.[3] In Morocco, Geertz's model might best apply to the merchants of the bazaars of Fez or Marrakesh, to their offshoots in the European sections of those towns, and to the cloth merchants along the Route de Strasbourg in Casablanca. Because of their roots in centuries-old practices Geertz sees these traders as the most likely source of economic innovation but also as inhibited by the weight of past practices. More specifically, these merchants lack not entrepreneurial skill but "the capacity to form efficient economic institutions; they are entrepreneurs without enterprises."[4]

The Swasa are not burdened with precedent or mercantile traditions; in terms of their own group almost all they have done has been unprecedented. Soussi trading in the north has been a direct function of the expansion of the European sections of Moroccan cities and the appearance and growth of a population of salaried consumers in urban areas. As such, their trading history goes back at best sixty years; many of those who started the Soussi "tradition" are still alive today in 1971.

The old Soussi *baqqalin* were fully integrated into a bazaar-type system in the medina-s of preprotectorate Morocco. But the egress of the older members of the Soussi communities from the native quarters of Fez and elsewhere to Tangier and Casablanca allowed a whole generation of Swasa (Hadj Brahim's generation) to skip the "stage" of bazaar trading. They went directly into retailing to European clientele, and when that market became overcrowded, the Swasa, equipped with new techniques, re-entered the native quarters, such as the Nouvelle Medina, and finally the shanty towns. They encountered a new sort of clientele con-

[3] *Ibid.* pp. 148–150.
[4] *Ibid.* pp. 28 and 74.

sisting of salaried laborers, bureaucrats, teachers, pensioned veterans, and the like, with fixed pay days. The new clientele had predictable amounts of disposable income, allowing the establishment of systematized credit buying. At the same time, the unemployed could barter services and favors for commodities, as had been the custom in the past.

Those mechanisms that the Swasa share with the bazaar traders have been, like all their other practices, consciously adopted because they seemed useful. By the same token, outworn methods can be, and have been, consciously discarded when their utility diminished. The Swasa's newness to trade would seem to provide them the potential for a great deal of innovative behavior. Hadj Abbid's taking out a life insurance policy in the 1920s may be a frivolous example, but it is nonetheless indicative of their openness to change. Whether in their capacity for innovation they differ significantly from the Fassi-s, whom one might suppose are more bound by their commercial traditions, I am not prepared to judge.

In the bazaar economy, the total flow of commerce is fragmented into a great number of unrelated, person-to-person transactions. There are myriad highly competitive commodity traders, and the system can absorb large numbers of people, but it turns the businessman away from long-term investment and the development of markets and towards petty speculation and short-run opportunism. Within this context the bazaar entrepreneur fails to organize coherent enterprises.[5] As noted in Chapter IV, the fragmentation and the proclivity towards speculation is not absent from the Moroccan retail system. On the other hand, the Swasa are capable of organizing enterprises. They have moved into cash farming, manufacturing, supermarkets, hotels and hotel chains, etc. As with so much else they do, they

[5] Ibid. p. 28.

engage in several kinds of behavior at once. They are capable of short-term opportunism (the Meknes cooking oil scandal) *and* long-term investment (Oulhadj's petroleum firm); *or* long-term speculation (the Casablanca tea barons). The little Soussi retailer is primarily a man out for steady gain, not a fast killing. The big Soussi is perfectly delighted to maximize all his options: steady gain, speculation, and the occasional big killing.

> The bazaar trader is unable to actively search out and create new sources of profit; he can only grasp occasions for gain as they fitfully and, from his point of view, spontaneously arise.[6]

Most of Hadj Brahim's pronouncements indicate a far less passive approach to trade on the part of the Swasa. In the 1930s, he and his fellows sought out customers door-to-door. Their European clientele knew them for immediate, reliable, and round-the-clock deliveries, and for stocking requested products. Their active entrepreneurship may be summed up by the saying: "The money of others is blind; you must use your own to guide it."

Two regulatory mechanisms operative in the bazaar model are a sliding price system and carefully managed credit relations. The sliding, or not fixed, character of commodity pricing places primary competitive stress between buyer and seller. *Ceteris paribus*, this analysis makes sense. In Casablanca and elsewhere in Morocco, there is a good deal of seller-buyer bargaining regarding the price of goods, the terms of credit, and black market transactions. At the same time there is intense seller-seller competition. It may arise, as among the Swasa, when they move, as many have moved,

[6] *Ibid.* p. 29.

to fixed prices on retail items. But it also reflects the over-crowding of the retail system, where the retailer must assure himself a steady clientele if he is to survive. The buyer is by no means a captive of the retailer; at least in the cities he can always go to another seller.

When Geertz deals with credit in the bazaar economy, we are on familiar ground. Credit does not simply make capital available to other entrepreneurs or to customers but is designed to "set up and stabilize more or less persisting commercial relationships." Recourse to public sources of credit is avoided, for "Private credit gives (the traders) more than simple access to capital; it secures their position in the flow of trade."[7] Clearly, this mechanism is central to Soussi practice, in which credit is the lifeblood of the distributive system, of wholesaler-retailer relations, of patrons and clients. It provides both moral and material cohesion to a physically dispersed community of Swasa within Casablanca and scattered through other cities. And the reliance upon private, in this case community, capital is still the norm. That norm may, however, be under some stress. Hadj Brahim laments the facile access to public credit that "everyone" has these days.[8] He is not condemning credit *per se*, for he has had access to and traded in credit all his life. What seems to disturb him is credit divorced from reputation; the resort to public credit is dangerous because it is depersonalized, and there will be no one to warn the unwary when they have gone in too deep. But more important, any extensive use of

[7] *Ibid.* p. 36.

[8] As Brahim intimated, the Soussi big men may go to the banks for credit. However, at lower levels the practice appears still to be rare. In 1968, analysts at the Banque de Crédit Populaire, specializing in small business loans, told me that their impression was that very few Soussi-s ever utilized the bank's facilities.

public credit would lead to the destabilization of those commercial-cum-community relationships mentioned by Geertz.

There are other "functional" aspects to the use of private credit in the distribution networks. The Swasa use community-bounded credit because, as mentioned earlier, it provides a fairly efficient apparatus for handling those who abuse the privilege. While one's Soussi-ness does not necessarily inspire trust in other Swasa, a notion of reliability is attached to one's status as a member of the group. Credit is not extended out of friendship or loyalty to the group, but out of the judgment that the borrower will use his credit wisely to maximize his own interests. Such judgments undoubtedly lie at the heart of the credit links between Jews and Swasa after the First World War and of patron-clientele chains among Soussi traders. As James Siegel noted with regard to Sumatran tradesmen, friendship and kinship have a utilitarian character; they are valuable as an index of a man's reliability. In precarious market conditions, it is seen as probable that a friend or kinsman will be the more reliable trader and the more responsible in his use of credit.[9]

Credit involves the question of how retailers and wholesalers estimate their returns on loans, their profits, and their assets. Not all earnings, and perhaps for the grocer-retailer not even most earnings, are monetized. Retailers among the indigenous population may accumulate favors as rapidly as cash. They may sell for cash or barter for other goods according to the client. In this context their total assets equal the sum of cash and stock on hand, property in the valley,

---

[9] Siegel, *Rope of God*, pp. 247–248. Siegel points out that, in contrast with the Swasa, the Atjehnese merchants of Sumatra prefer not to give credit to kinsmen, who might use such ties to delay repayment (p. 211).

promises of repayment, obligations, and favors, less their own debts and promised services to others. The Soussi grocer is not unique in this respect; he probably has counterparts throughout the Third World. One of the most sensitive studies of life in a North African village is Jean Duvignaud's *Chebika*, about a small oasis settlement in southern Tunisia. His portarit of Ridha, the village grocer, could easily be applied to many Moroccan retailers: [10]

> (Ridha) does possess a nest egg of sorts that he will never be able to capitalize fully, inasmuch as each repayment of credit impels a new extension. Ridha has developed a modern mentality, that of the merchant in a monetized economy, despite the fact that he handles only very small sums. ... He knows that in the form of labor on his land or the accumulation of services, he will eventually bring together some liquid assets that he can use in an independent manner.

In return for his "earnings," Ridha performs a service essential to the poor villagers: like the Soussi, he is willing to sell one match at a time and on credit.[11] Obligations are his major asset, and credit his major service.

In the bazaar economy, the successful entrepreneurs and the most daring innovators are from a group of traders

---

[10] Jean Duvignaud, *Chebika: Mutations dans un village du Maghreb* (Paris, 1968), p. 140. The English edition of the book is called *Change at Shebika*, (New York: Pantheon, 1970). All citations are from the French edition.

[11] *Ibid.* pp. 38–39, 53, 334. In this village, the peasants were greatly disturbed by rumors that the state might take over retail trade and run it through cooperatives. The thought of being in debt to the state and the probable need to buy, say, oil "a litre at a time" left the villagers in something of a panic. Ridha maintained his poise, realizing he would probably become manager of a cooperative if the state intervened.

combining religious asceticism with commercial frugality, at least in the Javanese town of Modjokuto. The local "big men" are frequently reformist. Muslims, spartan in their personal habits. These Calvinistic Muslims do accumulate capital, but they use it not for long-term investments but to cut in on a large number of profitable deals.[12] With Moroccan entrepreneurs—Swasa and Fassi-s alike—there are significant variations on the themes of piety and frugality, and the two are not necessarily paired. Hadj Brahim is a Muslim reformer and a frugal businessman, but at least in his reformism he is not typical of the Swasa. Yet the frugality of his urban life style and business habits are typical of all Soussi traders. Still, the frugality in business and consumption that leads to capital formation is situationally defined: one is frugal in the city to be opulent (in a relative sense) in the valley. Soussi-s are not Calvinistic through religious conviction, but because, given the goal of nurturing their local prestige, Calvinist habits make good sense. Moreover, there is a growing trend, for those who have the resources, to be opulent in the cities as well. Finally, to reiterate an earlier point, few Swasa would pass up the opportunity to sink accumulated capital into short-term speculation (the Toledano "crash" of 1959). They seem to have no "blinders" in their use of capital: their earnings may buy a citrus grove, or a trip to Mecca, or a house in the valley, or start a dry-cell battery factory, or acquire a rifle, or purchase a thousand litres of poisonous lubricants.

Both Geertz and Siegel stress that Javanese and Sumatran traders are able to insulate commercial ties from social relationships with friends and kin; that is, they can treat friends and kin on a strictly business basis.[13] The same

[12] Geertz, *Peddlers and Princes*, p. 39.
[13] *Ibid.* p. 46; and Siegel, *Rope of God*, p. 211.

phenomenon is evident among the Swasa: "We are brothers, but when it is time to do the accounts, we are enemies." I feel, however, that this insulation is not the breakdown in "ascriptive" ties that some Western sociologists in the Parsonian tradition see as leading to increased differentiation and role specialization in modern society. That brothers or kinsmen compete with one another does not mean that they are moving to the point where blood counts for relatively little. Cain and Abel were Middle Easterners, and a common feature of Middle Eastern society is conflict among brothers (or more distant relatives) in anticipation or as a result of the division of the father's patrimony. Fraternal conflict over material goods is nothing new, nor is competition among members of any ascriptive category, and until now at any rate, the Soussi category, or some subset of Soussi, has been useful for maintaining the accountability of individuals to one another, and, when necessary, for the application of sanctions.

The depersonalization of kinship ties in the commercial arena leads to an egalitarianism among participants. Kinship is not a basis of hierarchy. A framework for sanctions as a last resort, it does not justify continuous surveillance and control of the activities of kinsmen. Because there are, for instance, few salaried persons in the system, it is difficult to fire anyone. Even the apprentice or family aid labors in the expectation, which to date has been justified, that he will become an independent entrepreneur himself.[14] Hadj Brahim's frequent run-ins with his maternal uncle, at the ripe age of ten or eleven, amply demonstrate when deference plays second fiddle to ambition.

[14] The non-use of kinship to sustain authority relationships was suggested to me by Siegel's analysis of similar traits among the Atjehnese; *ibid.* p. 216.

In general, then, the Swasa share a number of attitudes and practices with the traders of Geertz's model of the bazaar economy. The Swasa, not coming from a traditional trading background, may be more free in their commercial behavior and more open to entrepreneurial innovation than the traders of Modjokuto (or the Fassi-s for that matter). This judgment, however, does not come to grips with the question of the long-run contribution such tradesmen, no matter how innovative, are likely to make to capital formation and economic development. Here the differences between Javanese and Soussi merchants become, in my view, much less significant. I share Geertz's conclusion that the impulse for economic development is not likely to come from these groups. "It is," Geertz warns, "romanticism or worse to suppose that the large-scale mobilization of human and natural resources needed for take-off can occur on a piecemeal, uncoordinated, laissez-faire basis . . . . To urge this sort of grass roots and small-industry policy on Indonesia . . . is to condemn her to wander in the no-man's land of transition indefinitely."[15] Yet romantics of this sort abound, and are nowhere more numerous than in the field of achievement motivation.

ACHIEVEMENT MOTIVATION, OR CAN HADJ BRAHIM SAVE THE MOROCCAN ECONOMY?

Over the past two decades social scientists have been more and more fascinated with achievement motivation as a key, if not *the* key, to economic development. We of the West are rich while most of the world is impoverished; we are superproductive while most of the world subsists or declines. Distribution of resources, available capital, climate, the nature of political systems, and other "common sense"

[15] Geertz, *Peddlers and Princes*, p. 156.

explanations can not account for the disparities in aggregate economic achievement across nations. David McClelland provides an explanation in his study *The Achieving Society*, with what might be called the "factor X" theory of economic growth: an indefinable psychological something that makes for efficient entrepreneurs. McClelland attempts to define factor X rigorously in terms of some individuals' need for achievement, an irrational motivation that the cultists refer to as n-ach.

The notion is that although the "externals" of growth may be present—capital, resources, manpower—without the *élan vital* of n-ach among commercial groups, nothing may happen. Further, even when the "externals" exist in reduced quantities, n-ach, strategically distributed, may save the day.[16]

> ... whether a country is developed or underdeveloped, poor or rich, industrial or agricultural, free or totalitarian ... men with high achievement motives will find a way to economic achievement. *What people want, they somehow manage to get* ... [emphasis added]

The hypothesis as stated is obviously irrefutable. If people have little, it either means that they wanted little in the first place or that they did not have the requisite level of n-ach to get what they want. The poor are poor because they are so motivated. The hypothesis is self-confirming, and, like one in economics that states "a man is paid what he is worth," morally blind. It is also irresponsibly romantic in suggesting that entrepreneurs with high n-ach can propel developing countries into the take-off stage. In McClelland's analysis Hadj Brahim, as an entrepreneurial type, is crucial to the growth of the Moroccan economy.

[16] McClelland, *Achieving Society*, p. 105.

The characteristic modes of behavior of the high n-achiever are that he or she sets moderate goals, prefers personal responsibility and control of the enterprise, desires feed-back on performance—typically monetary or material— and engages in research on the "environment" in which he or she is operating.[17] The high n-achiever does not seek monetary reward out of greed but as a barometer of success. For this reason one expects to find achievers concentrated among businessmen and entrepreneurs, although the theory allows for high n-achievers among bureaucrats and professional people. The activities of such people translate into economic growth because they are more concerned with expansion than with profits.[18]

I do not object to McClelland's argument that an empirically identifiable set of psychological motivations summarized as need-achievement exists—I accept that argument in its entirety—but rather to the implication McClelland feels n-ach holds for growth. One must ask how n-ach is stimulated in the first place, whether it can do what McClelland says it can do,[19] and finally, granting its efficacy,

[17] See David McClelland and D. Winter, *Motivating for Economic Development*, (Glencoe: Free Press, 1969), pp. 50–53.

[18] *Ibid.* p. 14. One wonders how the petty tradesmen of the developing countries, to the extent that they have n-ach, can gauge their performance if their assets and earnings are so frequently non-monetary.

[19] On this point, and it is a crucial one, McClelland has been methodologically evasive. Does n-ach *cause* growth, or is it simply an indicator that growth is taking place or that other factors making for growth are coming together? The notion of causality is vital to McClelland's thesis, for he recommends that we teach n-ach on the assumption of a causal link. (See McClelland and Winter, *Motivating*, throughout). Yet in his original formulation of the theory, McClelland waffles back and forth on this very point, sometimes suggesting causality, at others merely co-variance. See *The Achieving Society*, pp. 159, 203, 205, and 337. On p. 401, he even

is it desirable to inculcate n-ach in human beings? How the social scientist answers these questions will determine to some extent how we treat Hadj Brahim and others like him analytically and perhaps as objects of policy. Hadj Brahim conforms to many of the attributes of the high n-achiever. But what do we do with him? For somebody will try to manipulate the Hadj according to his own interpretation.

It is difficult to deal with the implications of n-ach because of the range of explanations of how its traits are stimulated in the first place. If, as we shall see, so many factors can produce it, perhaps it is not such a rare commodity after all. Some exploration of possible causes of n-ach may clarify the problems involved in determining its consequences.

McClelland in *The Achieving Society* is more concerned with measuring levels of n-ach in various societies than with speculating how it comes about. He finds strong statistical correlations between energy production and thematic achievement content in school books and folk tales. His basic point in both his 1961 and 1969 books is that children and adults can be educated to achieve by exposure to achievement themes and the achiever's way of thinking. How high n-achievers are spontaneously produced is of secondary concern to him.

Max Weber, although he never used the term n-ach, saw Western capitalist achievement as bound up with Protestantism and the Calvinist drive to prove one's favor in the eyes of God through economic achievement among men. Most subsequent theories of n-ach agree that Weber was on the right track but claim that he failed to realize that Protestantism encouraged child-rearing practices and early childhood training experiences conducive to adult achieve-

---

suggests that n-ach may bear a causal relationship to "political democracy."

ment motivation. E. E. Hagen has speculated that such child-rearing practices might develop disproportionately among groups suffering from status deprivation within their societies. Such groups—the Antiqueños of Colombia for instance—would undergo gradual change in family structure and parental attitudes towards children to stress early reliance training, a logical reward system for desired child behavior, and an emphasis on problem-solving. Finding normal routes to social standing blocked, these groups would move into undesirable trades—often in commerce or manufacturing—that the rest of society spurned. Religion, in this schema, plays a supportive but secondary role.[20]

Like many of the hypotheses we will review, this one tells us little about the Swasa. They do not feel rejected by the rest of society. They do resent Fassi condescension, but they are not alone in Morocco in putting up with it, and others experiencing that snobbism have not evidenced any particular entrepreneurial acumen. Nor does Weber's original hypothesis help us much, for the Swasa are all orthodox Sunni Muslims who feel themselves to be in the center of the Islamic traditions of Morocco. A combination of the theories of Hagen and Weber might apply to the entrepreneurial performance of the Jews of Morocco, but not to the Swasa.

Further, nothing, to my knowledge, distinguishes the Swasa from other Moroccans in terms of child-rearing practices. Early reliance training, central to many explanations of the development of n-ach, explains nothing about Soussi entrepreneurs. Soussi boys are put to a man's work at a very early age, separated from parents and siblings, and packed off great distances from their homes. This pattern, however, does not distinguish them from other Moroccan groups that

[20] See Hagen, *Theory*, throughout.

have not engaged in commerce. Throughout the countryside, Moroccan boys and girls are given full responsibility for
herding goats or sheep as soon as they are five years old.[21]
It has always impressed me that the children of the poor,
urban and rural, are on their own from an early age and
often responsible for some important function within the
family. There may be a major distinction between the reliance training of Hadj Brahim and that of thousands of other
Moroccan children of poor families, but it is not apparent
to me. From a different angle, students of n-ach point out
that its incidence is generally highest among members of
the middle and upper middle classes; yet I would hazard a
guess that in many countries of the Third World it is precisely this milieu in which parents are the most protective
of their children and in which reliance training is the least
stressed.

To add another wrinkle to those conditions conducive
to n-ach, James Siegel provides two important observations.
First, Atjehnese parents are indulgent towards their children, who are loved for, or in spite of, their lack of self-
control. Self-reliance and, equally important to n-ach theories, the postponement of gratification, are not inculcated
in children until adolescence. "What a boy learns in the
house is what it is not to be a male. . . . It is only outside the
house that he learns that the self-denial of instincts (*hawa
nafsu*) is what makes a boy an Atjehnese, a Muslim, and thus
a man."[22] Postponement of gratification is not part of the
development of achievement motivation at an early age, but
rather of a *rite de passage* to manhood, social status, and
religious fulfillment. Inasmuch as child-rearing practices

[21] See Paul Pascon, "Birth Control: Dialogue des Sourds,"
Lamalif, I, 3 (1966) 16–21.
[22] Siegel, *Rope of God*, p. 150.

would appear to have little influence on entrepreneurial proclivities among the Atjehnese, what does? Probably, Siegel suggests, the peculiar nature of husband-wife roles in Atjehnese society. Descent is bilateral (through both the male and female lines), and generally the female line retains possession of fixed assets such as land and houses. The husband, to maintain his own status and dignity within the family, must provide resources of his own: farming his wife's land is viewed as parasitic. The upshot is that many males migrate to trade in the "east." When asked about this phenomenon, villagers explain what would happen if the men did not trade. There would be lots of quarreling between husband and wife, she would ridicule him for not doing his share, and they would ultimately divorce. Therefore, for the sake of family harmony and self-respect, the husband must go off to trade.[23]

Along the same lines Leonard Kasdan became intrigued by E. E. Hagen's description of the Antiqueños, among whom are a large number of people of Basque origin. Could n-ach be an ethnic variable, in this case peculiar to the Basques? Kasdan answers affirmatively, for the Basques have an unusual system of marriage and inheritance that is not found elsewhere on the Iberian peninsula. Kasdan's hypothesis is that we can expect such variations to lead to predictable differences in character and personality.[24] Religion, reliance-training, problem-solving all drop away, and ethnicity and inheritance enter in as explanatory variables. Neither Siegel's nor Kasdan's analyses move us any closer to fathoming Soussi motivation.

[23] *Ibid.* p. 169.

[24] Leonard Kasdan, "Family Structure, Migration, and the Entrepreneur" *Comparative Studies in Society and History*, VII, 4 (1965) 345–357 (citation on p. 354).

One independent variable that might be directly related to n-ach levels in some societies is sex. The literature on the developing countries deals almost exclusively with male entrepreneurs. In several areas of West Africa, such as the cities of Accra and Lagos, over 80 percent of the petty traders are women.[25] The factor of sex, as it may affect commercial achievement, has been overlooked. Because among the Swasa female entrepreneurs are unheard of, I have paid scant attention to the role of sex in explaining Soussi behavior.

The Ibo of Eastern Nigeria have always seemed to me to resemble the Swasa in major respects. They have overpopulated their territory and outstripped their resources. They have practiced emigration for a generation or more and have become aggressive petty tradesmen throughout Nigeria. Some observers see their entrepreneurial skill as qualitatively different from that of neighboring ethnic groups: the Hausa and the Yoruba. Robert LeVine compares these three groups according to their levels of achievement motivation. On the basis of his data, he finds the Ibo to be the highest achievers of the three and posits that the systems of "status mobility" within the ethnic groups is the crucial variable. He rejects religion as a major factor because he finds no significant variation between Christian and Muslim subsamples within his Yoruba sample.[26] Because

[25] Kenneth Little, *West African Urbanization*, p. 124. A fascinating example of female commerce is that of the women of the Oulad Naïl of the pre-Saharan region of Algeria. Many of the women emigrate throughout the southern portions of Algeria as prostitutes, both before and during marriage, and thus, like the Swasa, are able to tap outside resources. The pattern is apparently quite ancient, and the commerce itself is not considered to be degrading. See Emile Dermenghem, *Le Pays d'Abel* (Paris, 1960).

[26] Robert LeVine, *Dreams and Deeds: Achievement Motivation in Nigeria* (University of Chicago Press, 1966), pp. 58–59.

mobility among the Hausa is determined, according to LeVine, by kinship and economic clientage, a premium is placed upon subservience, and independent, innovative behavior is not rewarded. In direct contrast, attaining status in Ibo society is much more dependent upon a man's individual occupational achievement than upon his blood or patrons. The Yoruba lie somewhere in between the Hausa and Ibo in terms of their status mobility and thus their achievement levels. LeVine's causal chain runs like this: *status mobility system→ parental values→ child-rearing practices→ personality frequencies including n-ach.*[27]

What LeVine discerns as unique in the Ibo status mobility system is best summarized in his citation of an article by Simon Ottenberg:[28]

> The possibilities of enhancing status and prestige are open to virtually all individuals except descendants of certain types of slaves and are not restricted to members of particular lineages, clans or other social units. Ibo society is thus, in a sense, an "open society" in which positions of prestige, authority and leadership are largely achieved.

This statement could be applied to Moroccan society in its entirety. Although it may help us understand why Ibos are higher achievers than Hausa, it cannot answer why some Moroccans are higher achievers than others within the same status mobility system.

But even in terms of the Hausa-Ibo dichotomy LeVine sets forth, he is not entirely convincing. "One point which

[27] *Ibid.* pp. 18–19.
[28] Simon Ottenberg, "Ibo Receptivity to Change" in Bascom and Herskovits, eds, *Continuity and Change in African Cultures,* (University of Chicago Press, 1958) pp. 136–37; cited by LeVine, *Dreams and Deeds,* p. 32.

is entirely clear," he states, "is that the Hausa status system was politically oriented, whereas the Ibo one was occupationally oriented."[29] This judgment does not mesh, however, with an earlier observation that Ibo big men did not have to rely on kinship for status because with earned wealth they could purchase guns and gunpowder and attract a following thereby.[30] If that is not political clientage in its crudest form, then I do not know what is. It is also highly reminiscent of the early big men from the Anti-Atlas. As both the Swasa and Ibo demonstrate, there is no reason why clientage must necessarily entail subservience.

When LeVine brings into play such variables as political systems, he begins to approach, perhaps inadvertently, my own view of the emergence of n-ach and the constraints upon its ultimate impact upon the economy. The politico-economic situation in which the potential entrepreneur operates must be fully understood, for the achiever will not achieve regardless of the situation in which he finds himself. Further, chance situational phenomena may influence the emergence of n-achievers as much as status deprivation, ethnicity, reliance training, etc. We may all be, as Cyril Belshaw contends, achievers of a sort, but how manifest our motivations may be will depend on how we perceive the obstacles to success and what goals we set for ourselves. Along these lines economic determinism confronts the "little man" theory of history.

The broad situational backdrop that I see for the question of entrepreneurship and the calculation of risk in the developing countries is fundamental economic scarcity with an overlay of unstable and unpredictable government. In this context "rational" economic behavior may be to maxi-

[29] *Ibid.* p. 36.
[30] *Ibid.* p. 34.

mize one's advantage by *minimizing* one's risks. The situation is hardly conducive to the kinds of initiatives and positive risks that we associate with entrepreneurial behavior. In fact, the high n-achiever in this situation might be the person most skilled at limiting his risks, ensuring that he stands to lose less than others rather than gain more. If the situation were altered in a major way, if access to new resources opened up, if capital became readily available, if stable markets were developed, if political considerations became less relevant to economic success, *then* one might find large numbers of people manifesting the attributes of high n-achievers. Opportunities in situations of scarcity, I would argue, create the achieving man, and not the other way around.

Substantial populations of latent achievers may not channel their motivations into growth because the situation in which they must take their first risks is too forbidding. McClelland himself has affirmed time and again that the high n-achiever is most productive in situations of *moderate* uncertainty, or where he has about a fifty-fifty chance of success.[31] It would be interesting to know how many Third World countries McClelland thinks offer odds as favorable as fifty-fifty. The real odds in these countries can easily reduce anyone with entrepreneurial inclinations to the kind of day-to-day hedonism vividly depicted by Oscar Lewis as characteristic of the culture of poverty.[32]

The people of the Tunisian village of Chebika live in utter poverty amidst crumbling houses alongside an oasis

[31] McClelland, *Achieving Society*, p. 211 and McClelland and Winter, *Motivating*, pp. 16 and 338.

[32] See Oscar Lewis, "The Culture of Poverty" *Scientific American*, CCXV, 4 (October, 1966) 19–25; and *La Vida* (Vintage Books, 1968), pp. xliii–lii.

that they do not own but merely sharecrop. At first blush, the villagers appeared stoically resigned to their destitution, yet over time it became apparent to Duvignaud and his colleagues that they wanted to work for the prosperity of the village and to rebuild it. The villagers were convinced that the government in Tunis had to give them the wherewithal to get started. They literally had nothing with which to begin. In the meantime they waited for something to happen, for the government to step in.[33] Are these low achievers who *believe* they have no control over their fate? Or could they be potentially high achievers who *in fact* have little control over their fate?

A sample of Moroccan rural youth frequently invested what they earned in clothes, cigarettes, an occasional bottle of wine, or an even less frequent visit to a brothel. The notion of self-improvement and building for the future through hard work seemed totally foreign to these young men. Yet in respone to the question "Suppose you had 10 dirhams (5 dirhams equals a dollar); 50 dirhams; 2,500 dirhams; 10,000 dirhams; what would you do with the money?"[34] 320 of them answered as follows:

How it would be spent	10 dh.	50 dh.	2,500 dh.	10,000 dh.
		(in percent)		
clothes, personal care	48	32	14	9
leisure	20	22	8	7
helping family, food	8	13	12	8
savings and investment	2	22	52	54
charity	4	0	0	12
other, no answer	18	11	14	10

[33] Duvignaud, *chebika*, p. 303.

[34] Paul Pascon and Mekki Bentahar, "Ce que disent 296 jeunes ruraux" *Bulletin Economique et Social du Maroc*, XXXI, 112–113 (1969) 1–145; table on p. 92.

Although declared intentions are not a sure guide to what the respondents would actually do with large sums of money, they indicate that their habits of self-gratification are a function of low income and would change towards savings and investment if they had assets to make such behavior feasible.

Of course, McClelland and other students of n-ach have faced the argument of situational determinism and found it wanting. The beauty of their counterarguments for the Western policy maker, the stability-oriented social scientist, and the local potentate is that they appear to have a magic formula for economic growth without political upheaval and planned economic transformation. The theory would urge governments to worry less about capital formation, taxation, land reform, nationalization, and political participation and invest relatively small sums in introducing achievement themes into school books and in-career achievement training seminars for entrepreneurs.[35] To seal their argument, McClelland and Winter state that whatever the situation or incentive structure, response to incentives will always be differential within and across populations, and that sensitivity to new opportunities may be governed by achievement levels.[36] The Swasa, it could be argued, represent that differential response to opportunity that McClelland and Winter have in mind. But it is a long step from this observation to the conclusion that the structure of rewards and opportunities is of secondary importance. Hadj Brahim tells us that the Arabs from the countryside around Casa-

[35] See McClelland and Winter for their rebuttal of classical economic theory and their belittling of the importance of "getting politicians and government leaders to do what they ought to do . . . ," *Motivating*, p. 5.
[36] *Ibid.*, p. 9.

blanca looked at the city without seeing the opportunities that it contained. But although it may have taken some time, they see *now*. The growth of Casablanca created a situation favorable to the Swasa, and they took quick advantage of it. But if the situation becomes less favorable to them, as appears to be the case now, they may abandon the city, or trade, or both. The growth of Casablanca depended on massive French investment, not local investment. The city in turn made the Soussi entrepreneur, but he is relatively helpless to save the city.

One is still confronted with the difficulty of explaining the successful entrepreneurial outburst of the Soussi core tribes. The existential reality of the poverty of their homeland, mediated and intensified by introverted conflicts and struggles for local status and prestige, pushed the Swasa to the north. The commercial savvy of the pioneers, like Hadj Brahim's father, did not create their initial success, but rather the fact that they *happened* to be the right people at the right time. Other Moroccans could just as easily have made the move into commerce, but the luck of the draw produced the Swasa. And even then a number of Soussi tribes, differing in no significant way from the core tribes, migrated as miners and factory workers. There is nothing magic about commerce; the people of the Ammiln could as easily be working in the Renault plants in France as in the grocery stores of Casablanca. The argument that high n-achievers often take up commercial pursuits the better to measure their performance does not hold in this instance, for then one would expect *all* tribes of the Sous to be in trade.[37] The Swasa simply do whatever they have to do to

[37] Daniel Noin calls our attention to the Ida ou Nadif of the Anti-Atlas, who, through the luck of the draw, emigrated to Marrakesh as artisans, slipper-makers (*babouchiers*). There is no social,

draw on outside resources. In fact, if tribes like the Ida Gwagmar, continue to "over-achieve" in factory labor in France, we may see young Swasa abandoning commerce to become laborers in France. At the same time, tribes known for labor migration, such as the eastern Riffis of northern Morocco or the Ait Souab neighboring the Ammiln, are increasingly drifting into trade. I am tempted by the notion that if opportunities are held constant for the entire Moroccan population, the Swasa will probably be faster off the mark than most other groups in seizing them. But opportunities are not constant across the entire population, nor do all groups operate under the same constraints and economic handicaps. When resources, policies, opportunities, and rewards are distributed evenly throughout the Moroccan population, then perhaps the Swasa will make a disproportionate contribution to growth. Until then, the situation is far beyond their control or influence. Hadj Brahim will not save the Moroccan economy.

The situation is beyond the control of entrepreneurs in many countries of the Third World, for the tasks of stimulating growth are too monumental to be undertaken by private individuals. These tasks must be undertaken by central governments, whose success or failure may in turn depend on a fairly drastic redistribution of wealth among the rich and poor nations. Many developing countries are in any case so far committed to state-guided growth that little room is left for entrepreneurs to have any impact. The liberal capitalist systems with ample resources (their own or imported) that might be hospitable to entrepreneurs with

---

structural, ecological, status, or religious factor that could distinguish the Ida ou Nadif from the Ammiln. Noin, *Population Rurale*, II, 207.

high n-ach will most probably never be a feature of the Third World.

Should we lament this fact? Despite repeated disclaimers that achievement theory is not culture-specific,[38] one cannot help feeling that the advocates of n-ach would populate the world with Connecticut Yankees. These innovative, dynamic, problem-solving, nature-mastering individuals may be associated with more than rising curves of electrical power production or growth in GNP; perhaps in the aggregate they are associated with the expansionist tendencies of capitalist economies. McClelland measures levels of achievement and the economic vitality of ancient Athens and sixteenth century Spain through the growth of their empires.[39] Does he regard the Anglo-Saxon empires of the nineteenth and twentieth centuries as yet another expression of healthy levels of n-ach in the English-speaking world?

What manner of beast is the high n-achiever? For his admirers, someone who should not be thwarted, who must be encouraged to play out his own hard-nosed race with himself. LeVine, in a jarring statement, reveals the extremes to which n-ach can carry those deeply imbued with it or taken with its uncovering and analysis. Referring to the Ibo-engineered *coup d'état* in Nigeria in 1966, he isolates its cause: "It was the voice of achievement striving in the form of political ideology taken more seriously by the Ibo than by other groups."[40]

The high n-achiever, so we are told, in order to influence economic growth must be low in an attribute called

---

[38] McClelland and Winter, *Motivating*, pp. 26–28.
[39] McClelland, *Achieving Society*, p. 117.
[40] LeVine, *Dreams and Deeds*, p. 77.

n-affiliation, or the need to maintain friendly relations with other people. Conforming to group standards and worrying unduly about one's relations with others will tend to discourage the impersonal, and if need be, ruthless ventures that are the high n-achiever's hallmark.[41]

With regard to n-affiliation, Hadj Brahim is very much a transitional figure. The rationality and impersonality that the high n-achiever introduces into his commercial activities run counter to the n-affiliation, the adherence to social patterns and norms, that typify societies with scarce resources, spotty administration, and incipient market economies (in my way of thinking it is this cluster of factors that commonly evokes the label "traditional" although "modern" societies could relapse into a similar mold). Hadj Brahim balks at rationalization and consolidation; not because he cannot understand the economic advantages contained therein, but because he sees the social costs involved. He sees the opportunities for manipulation and exploitation in the n-achiever's economic behavior, but he sometimes, although not always, shies away from seizing them. We can compare Hadj Brahim with Hassan, a Bedouin, living in his tents near the village of Chebika. Duvignaud found the Bedouin to be the only people in the area with what we would call manifest achievement motivation. Hassan in particular sees everything in terms of earnings, and he decides that marrying off his sister will cost him too much in dowry, depriving him of investments for his fields and flocks. The girl suffers from epilepsy, a condition that has been regarded in rural society as reflecting a person's special relation to God. Hassan resolves to capitalize on this folk

[41] LeVine uses a dimension called Obediance-Social Compliance (OSC) to contrast the Hausa, who are high in it, with the Ibo who are low. *Ibid.* p. 68.

resource and encourages people to come and see his sister in her capacity as seer and intercessor with the divine. If Hassan's calculated exploitation of others, including a family member, leads to capital formation, must we applaud his act? Hadj Brahim might act similarly, but then again he might not. His norms lead him, it seems to me, to fear the directions in which he sees himself and others like him, heading. He occasionally draws back. The question is, should he be encouraged to become consistent? Should he be encouraged to abandon traditional forms of exploitation *and* traditional forms of social interaction that have low economic payoff in order to sharpen his quest for entrepreneurial excellence? McClelland presumably would say "Yes," on the assumption that such consistency leads in the aggregate to economic growth.[42]

Perhaps fortunately for Hadj Brahim, he is doomed to play an ancillary role in economic development. If it occurs

[42] Duvignaud, *Chebika*, p. 195. McClelland is occasionally cognizant of the seamier side of n-ach. Interculturally, positive responses to the item from Adorno's F-scale on authoritarianism, dealing with gratitude and respect for parents, correlate most highly with levels of n-ach. This item is associated with people who are socially and politically conservative, personally rigid, and racist; McClelland, *Achieving Society*, p. 254. I was personally struck by a chart in John Gillin's study of a Guatemalan town, that listed the psychological attributes of the dominant Ladino caste and the subordinate Indian caste in the town. The Ladinos manifest a future-oriented, problem-solving, instrumental outlook on life while the Indians are passive, complying to forces of nature and the divine, and existing in a "timeless present." But I suppose that McClelland might argue that if the Indians wanted anything more than their current status, they could have gotten it, while the more highly motivated Ladinos have what they deserve. See John Gillin, *The Culture of Security in San Carlos: A Study of a Guatemalan Community of Indians and Ladinos*, Middle America Research Institute (New Orleans: Tulane, 1951), p. 121.

at all, he and the Swasa will not be its motor force. That force will come from state planning and public capital formation, international aid-granting bodies, foreign corporate investers, political revolution, or a combination of all the above. Hadj Brahim and the Swasa may survive the economic change represented by these factors but will have relatively little impact upon them. For it to be otherwise, they, like the Ibos, would have to infiltrate the professions, the army, and the bureaucracy, where they would become part of the decision-making elite. But then we would no longer be dealing with the Soussi phenomenon depicted throughout these pages. Trading in the north, like farming in the valley, would become a relic of the Soussi past, a milestone on their progress towards elite status, where they would no longer be a cog in someone else's grand design but the designers themselves. Hadj Brahim will certainly not make the transition, but it may be well within the grasp of his children.

Appendix

Distribution of Soussi Tradesmen in the North (According to Hadj Brahim)

CASABLANCA: the great majority are from the Ammiln

RABAT: the majority are from Tasserirt and Amanouz (near the Ammiln)

MARRAKESH: dominated by the Ida ou Gnidif

MEKNES: dominated by the Ida ou Gnidif

TANGIER: many Ammiln, mostly from Afelli-wasif. There are more and more Riffi-s

SETTAT: Ammiln, mostly from the Agounsi-wasif

AL-JADIDA: Ammiln, mostly from the Agounsi-wasif

ESSAOUIRA: practically no Swasa, mostly people from the Haha

FEZ: Igounane and Ait Tafrawt (Ammiln)

SEFROU: Ida ou Gnidif

TAZA: mostly Ammiln from the Afelli-wasif

BEN AHMAD: Ida ou Semlal

TETOUAN: there is not a single Soussi at Tetouan

KSAR AL-KEBIR: Ammiln from the Ait Smayoun

LARACHE: Ammiln dominant

SOUK AL-ARBA: Ammiln mostly from the Agounsi-wasif

KENITRA: Ammiln mostly from the Ait Smayoun

OUJDA: there are no Swasa at Oujda

SAFI: there are Swasa but many Arabs as well

SALÉ: Ida ou Zekri

Hadj Brahim specified that his listing does not mean that all grocers in these towns are from the tribes cited, but rather that the dominant group is.

Glossary

The Core Tribes of the Sous

Ammiln
Ida ou Gnidif
Amanouz-Tasserirt
Ait Baha
Ait Wadrim
Ait Mzal
Ida ou Ktir
Ait Souab

Other Tribes of the Sous mentioned in the text

Ait Abdullah
Ida Gersmouk
Ida ou Ba'aqil
Ida ou Semlal
Ida ou Gwagmar
Ait Ba'amrane
Tazeroualt (more a region than a tribe. Its center is the saintly
    village of Sidi Ahmad ou Moussa)

Tribes of the Ammiln

Ait Tafrawt
Tahala
Afelli-wasif
Agounsi-wasif
Ait Smayoun
Ida ou Milk

Villages of the Ammiln mentioned in the text

Iskouzrou
Adday

Addad
Aguerdoudad
Anameur
Tahala
Tafrawt
Taguenza

Other Tribes Mentioned

Jebala   Western Rif Mountains
Chawia   Casablanca hinterland
Dukkala   al-Jadida hinterland
Chiadma   Safi hinterland
Haha   Essaouira hinterland

Abbreviations

FDIC   Front pour la Défense des Institutions Constitu-
        tionelles
UMCIA   Union Marocaine des Commerçants, Industriels et
        Artisans
UMGPA   Union Marocaine des Grossistes en Produits
        Alimentairs
UMT   Union Marocaine du Travail
UNFP   Union Nationale des Forces Populaires
COSUMA Compagnie Sucrière Marocaine

Terms

adloun (Berber)   a sort of tambourine
afus; ifassen (Berber)   lit. hand, but used to mean lineage
agadir (Berber)   a fortified communal storehouse. Also the
     name of a major city in the Sous: Agadir
agillas; igillassen (Berber, derived from Arabic)   lit. sitter,
     used to mean shop manager
ahwash (Berber)   a Soussi dance form
ait al-mal (Berber-Arabic)   wholesalers
akhadam (Berber derived from Arabic)   a day laborer

akhourbiche (Berber)   the area of the mosque in which water
    is heated for ablutions
'alim; 'ulema' (Arabic)   religious jurists
amashghal (Berber derived from Arabic)   day laborer
amghar; imgharen (Berber)   leader of a tribe; after 1934, title
    of men appointed by French to administer a village
amqun (Berber)   tribal alliance
anflous; inflassen (Berber)   tribal leader at level of lineage
anfugour; infugourn (Berber)   a leader at the *afus* level
argan (Berber)   tree peculiar to the Sous
'attar (Arabic)   spice seller

bab-tigemmi (Berber-Arabic)   head of the household
bab-nchi (Berber-Arabic)   shopowner
baqqal; baqqalin (Arabic)   grocers of a traditional kind
bisri (Berber-Arabic derived from French épicerie)   a modern
    grocery
bled (Arabic)   the countryside

dhimmi (Arabic)   a Jew or a Christian—a protected person
diya (Arabic)   blood money
douar (Arabic)   a village

fqih (Arabic)   a religious instructor
funduq (Arabic)   a hotel or caravansary

hanout (Arabic)   shop; berberized to give tahannout
harka (Arabic)   a military levy; berberized to give harkth

inkiri (Berber derived from Arabic)   a shepherd by contract

jellaba (Arabic)   an ankle-length outer garment for men

kaftan (Arabic)   woman's outer garment
kanoun; takath (Arabic and Berber)   a hearth or a household
kissaria (Arabic derived from Latin)   cloth bazaar

lantar (Berber)   a sort of banjo
leftida (Berber derived from Arabic)   to redeem property
    temporarily sold

lehri (Arabic)   a warehouse

luh (Berber from Arabic)   a tribal code

luha (Arabic)   the plank upon which children write Koran verses

mahal (Arabic)   lit. place, but also a shop

makhzan (Arabic)   storehouse, but in Morocco it refers to the government

ma'llim (Arabic)   lit. one who teaches, but used to designate a patron or boss

masherkil (Berber derived from Arabic)   an associate in business

medina (Arabic)   a city; in Morocco, the old and/or native quarter of the city

mellah (Arabic)   the quarter reserved for the Jews in various Moroccan cities

mit'allim (Arabic)   an apprentice

moussem (Arabic)   the annual pilgrimage to the tomb of a saint

muda' (Berber derived from Arabic)   a village agglomeration

mul al-hanout (Arabic)   shopowner or proprietor

muqaddim (Arabic) generally an official in a city quarter

naqus (Arabic)   a bell or gong; in the Sous, a piece of metal

qa'id (Arabic)   a government official at the district level

qadiyya (Arabic)   used by Hadj Tahar to indicate something legal according to *shari'a*

rais (Arabic)   a head or chief; in the Sous, the man who leads the *ahwash*

rba' (Arabic)   a fourth; a level of tribal organization between clan and village

rbab (Arabic)   a one-stringed violin

rqass (Arabic)   a courier

ruwassi; ruwassa (Arabic)   a married man living without his wife

shari'a (Arabic)   the body of Islamic law
sheikh (Arabic)   an official at the village level
simsar (Arabic)   a broker
siroual (Arabic)   baggy pants or bloomers

tafgurt (Berber)   the levying of fines
talib; tulba (Arabic) lit. students; in the Sous, those learned in
    Islam
tanouramt (Berber)   credit
thagalit (Berber)   oath-swearing
timzgida (Berber derived from Arabic)   a mosque
tunya (Berber)   the act of selling land or property temporarily
tusherka (Berber from Arabic)   partnership or association

'urf (Arabic)   customary law

wadi (Arabic)   anything from a streambed to a river valley

xzin (Berber from Arabic)   a storehouse or depot

zawiya (Arabic)   lit. a corner; refers to the physical locales of
    religious orders

Bibliography

Adam, André. *Casablanca: Essai sur la transformation de la société marocaine au contact de l'Occident*. Paris: CNRS, 1968. 2 vols.

———. "Le 'bidonville' de Ben M'sik à Casablanca," *Annales de l'Institut d'Etudes Orientales*, VIII (1949–50).

———. "La maison et le village dans quelques tribus de l'Anti-Atlas," *Hespéris*, XXXVII (1950).

Alport, E. A. "The Ammiln," *Journal of the Royal Anthropological Institute*, XCIV, 2 (1964).

———. "The Mzab," *Journal of the Royal Anthropological Institute*, LXXXIV (1954).

Ardener, Shirley. "The Comparative Study of Rotating Credit Associations," *Journal of the Royal Anthropological Institute*, XCIV, 2 (1964).

Belshaw, Cyril E. *Traditional Exchange and Modern Markets*. Englewood Cliffs, N.J.: Prentice-Hall, 1965.

Benech, José. *Essai d'explication d'un Mellah*. Private printing in Germany, n.d..

Bernard, Stéphane. *Le Conflit Franco-Marocain: 1943–1956*. Brussels, 1963. 3 vols.

Berque, Jacques. *Structures Sociales du Haut-Atlas*. Paris: PUF, 1955.

Berrada, Ghali. "L'entrepreneur marocain: une élite de transition." Thèse pour le Doctorat d'Etat en sciences economiques, Université de Bordeaux, 1968.

Bourdieu, Pierre, et al. *Le Métier de Sociologue: Livre 1*. Paris: Mouton, 1968.

Bousquet, G. H. *Ibn Khaldoun: Les Textes sociologiques et économiques de la Muqaddima*. Paris, 1965.

Brignon, Jean, et al. *Histoire du Maroc*. Casablanca, 1967.

Chaumeil, Jean. "Le mellah de Tahala au pays des Ammeln," *Hespéris*, XL (1953).

———. "Histoire d'une tribu maraboutique de l'Anti-Atlas: les Ait Abdullah ou Said," *Hespéris*, XXXIX (1952).

Chenier, L. *The Present State of the Empire of Morocco*. New York: Johnson Reprint, 1967. 2 vols.

Chraibi, Driss. *Le Passé Simple*. Paris, 1954.

———. *Succession Ouverte*. Paris: Denoel, 1962.

Coatalen, Paul. "Reflexions sur la société chleuh," *Annales Marocaines de Sociologie* (1969).

Coleman, J. S. *Community Conflict*. Glencoe: Free Press, 1956.

Coser, Lewis. *The Functions of Social Conflict*. Glencoe: Free Press, 1964.

Cohen, Abner. *Custom and Politics in Urban Africa: A Study of Hausa Migrants in Yoruba Towns*. Berkeley and Los Angeles: University of California Press, 1969.

DeFleurieu, Capt. "Une tribu des commerçants berbères au sud du Maroc: les Ammeln," Paris: Centre de Hautes Etudes sur l'Afrique et l'Asie Moderne, III, 45 bis (1939); unpublished, 14 pp.

De la Porte des Veaux, Cne. "L'émigration dans le Sous," Paris: Centre de Hautes Etudes sur l'Afrique et l'Asie Moderne, 1556 (1948–1949); unpublished, 75 pp.

Delisle, S. *L'Evolution sociale du Maroc*. Paris, 1951.

De Perigny, Maurice. *Au Maroc: Fès la capitale du Nord*. Paris, 1917.

Dermenghem, Emile. *Le Culte des Saints dans l'Islam maghrébin*. Paris, 1954.

———. *Le Pays d'Abel*. Paris, 1960.

Duvignaud, Jean. *Chebika: Mutations dans un village du Maghreb*. Paris, 1968.

———. *Change at Shebika* (English translation) New York: Pantheon, 1970.

Festinger, Leon. *A Theory of Cognitive Dissonance*. Row, Peterson, 1957.

Flamand, Pierre. *Les communautés israélites du Sud-Marocain.* Casablanca, n.d. (1951?).

Forbes, Rosita. *El-Raisuni: The Sultan of the Mountains.* London, 1924.

Gaillard, Henri. *Une Ville de l'Islam: Fès.* Paris, 1905.

Galand-Pernet, Paulette. "Poésie berbère du Sud du Maroc et 'motifs économiques'," in Berque, J. and Charnay, J.-P., eds., *De l'Impérialisme à la Décolonisation.* Paris, 1965.

Geertz, Clifford. *Islam Observed: Religious Development in Morocco and Indonesia.* Yale University Press, 1968.

———. "In Search of North Africa," *New York Review of Books*, XVI, 7, (April 22, 1971).

———. *Peddlers and Princes: Social Change and Economic Modernization in two Indonesian Towns.* University of Chicago Press, 1963.

———. "The Rotating Credit Association: A Middle Rung in Development," *Economic Development and Cultural Change* (April, 1962).

Gellner, Ernest. *Saints of the Atlas.* London: Weidenfeld and Nicolson, 1969.

———. "Pendulum Swing Theory of Islam," in Roland Robertson, ed., *Sociology of Religion*, Baltimore: Penguin, 1969.

Gillin, John. *The Culture of Security in San Carlos: A Study of a Guatemalan Community of Indians and Ladinos.* Middle America Research Institute. New Orleans: Tulane, 1951.

Hagen, E. E. *On the Theory of Social Change.* Dorsey Press, 1962.

Justinard, Col. *Le Caïd Goundafi.* Casablanca, 1951.

———. *Notes sur l'Histoire du Sous au XVIe Siècle.* Archives Marocaines, Paris, XXIX (1933).

———. "Les chleuh de la banlieue de Paris," *Revue des Etudes Islamiques* II (1928).

———. *Les Aït Ba'amrane.* Villes et Tribus du Maroc, XIII.

Kasdan, Leonard. "Family Structure, Migration, and the Entrepreneur," *Comparative Studies in Society and History*, VII, 4 (1965).

Kingdom of Morocco. *La consommation et les depens des ménages marocains musulmans*. Rabat: Service Central des Statistiques, 1961.

————. *Recensement Démographique*. Rabat: Service Central des Statistiques, 1962–1963. Several volumes.

————. *Enquête à Objectifs multiples: 1961–1963*. Rabat: Service Central des Statistiques, 1964.

————. *Etude sur le Commerce Intérieur*. Rabat: Division des Statistiques et du Plan, 1968. 3 vols.

Lahlou, Abdelouahab. "Notes sur la banque et les moyens d'échanges commerciaux à Fès avant le Protectorat," *Hespéris*, XXIV (1937).

LeTourneau, Roger. *Fès avant le Protectorat*. Casablanca, 1949.

LeVine, Robert A. *Dreams and Deeds: Achievement Motivation in Nigeria*. University of Chicago Press, 1966.

Lewis, Oscar. "The Culture of Poverty," *Scientific American*, CCXV, 4 (October, 1966).

————. *La Vida*. Vintage Books, 1968.

Maneville, Cdt.R. "Prolétariat et bidonvilles," Paris: Centre de Hautes Etudes sur l'Afrique et l'Asie Moderne, LXIII, 1712 (1950); unpublished.

Marquez, G. "Les épiciers chleuhs et leur diffusion dans les villes du Maroc," *Bulletin Economique et Social du Maroc*, II (1935).

Massignon, Louis. *Enquête sur les corporations Muselmanes d'artisans et de comerçants au Maroc*. Paris, 1925.

McClelland, David. *The Achieving Society*. Glencoe: Free Press, 1967.

———— and Winter, D. *Motivating for Economic Development*. Glencoe: Free Press, 1969.

Miège, J.-L. *Le Maroc et l'Europe*. Paris, 1962. 4 vols.

————. "Origine et développement de la consommation du

thé au Maroc," *Bulletin Economique et Social du Maroc*, XX, 71 (1956).

Montagne, Robert. *Les Berbères et le Makhzen dans le Sud du Maroc*. Paris, 1930.

———— *Naissance du Prolétariat Marocain*. Paris, 1950.

Monteil, Vincent. "Choses et gens du Bani," *Hespéris*, XXXIII (1946).

Montjean, H. "L'émigration dans le Sous," Paris: Centre de Hautes Etudes sur l'Afrique et l'Asie Moderne, XXVI, 639 (1942); unpublished.

Mosel, James. "Communication Patterns and Political Socialization in Translational Thailand," in Lucien Pye, ed., *Communications and Political Development*. Princeton University Press, 1967.

Nelson, Joan. *Migrants, Urban Poverty, and Instability in Developing Nations*. Cambridge, Mass.: C.I.A., Harvard University Press, 1969.

Noin, Daniel. *Casablanca*. Rabat: Atlas du Maroc, 1965.

———— *La Population rurale du Maroc*. Rouen: PUF, Université de Rouen, 1970. 2 vols.

Pascon, Paul. "Birth Control: Dialogue des sourds," *Lamalif*, I, 3 (1966).

———— and Trystram, J. P. "L'émigration des Chleuhs du Souss: les Ait-Ouadrim à Jerada," *Bulletin Economique et Social du Maroc*, XVIII, 62 (1954).

Rokeach, Milton. "Attitude Change and Behavioral Change," *Public Opinion Quarterly*, XXX, 4 (Winter 1966–1967).

Salmon, G. "Le commerce indigène à Tanger," Archives Marocaines, Paris, I (1904).

Siegel, James T. *The Rope of God*. Berkeley and Los Angeles: University of California Press, 1969.

Stone, Russell. "The Djerbian Ethic: Correlates of the Spirit of Capitalism in Tunisia." Paper presented at the fourth annual meeting of the Middle East Studies Association, Columbus, Ohio, November 6, 1970.

Tharaud, Jerome and Jean. *Fès, ou les bourgeois de l'Islam.* Paris, 1930.

Vie Economique (La). Numéro spécial: "Les industries alimentaires," December, 1967.

Vinogradov, A. and Waterbury, J. "Situations of Contested Legitimacy: Morocco—An Alternative Framework," *Comparative Studies in Society and History*, XIII, 1 (January, 1971).

Waterbury, John. *The Commander of the Faithful: The Moroccan Political Elite—A Study in Segmented Politics.* London and NYC: Weidenfeld and Nicolson and Columbia University Press, 1970.

———— "Les détaillants Souassa à Casablanca," *Bulletin Economique et Social du Maroc*, XXXI, 114 (1969).

Waterbury, John. "Tribalism, Trade and Politics—the Transformation of the Swasa of Morocco," in Gellner, Ernest and Micaud, Charles, eds., *Arabs and Berbers: Ethnicity and Nation-Building in North Africa.* Forthcoming, 1972.

Westermarck, Edward. *Wit and Wisdom in Morocco: A Study of Native Proverbs.* London, 1930.

Yacine, Katib. "J'ha" in *Mars* (Union National des Etudiants Marocains). Rabat, n.d. (March, 1969?).

Zerdoumi, Nefissa. *Enfants d'hier: l'éducation de l'enfant en milieu traditionnel algérien.* Paris: Maspéro, 1970.

Index